The **Mini Rough Guide** to

IRELAND

How to download your Free eBook

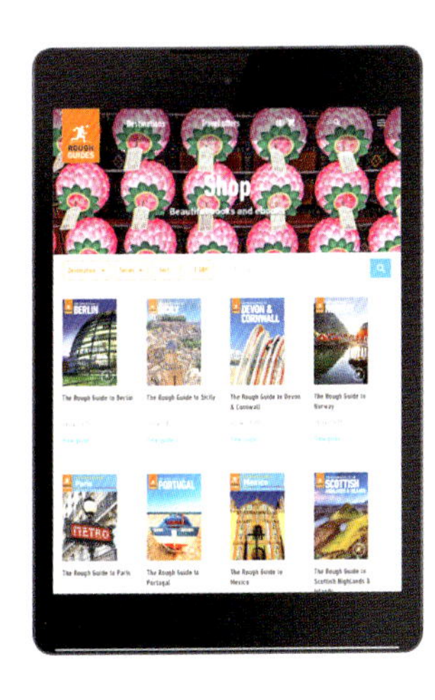

1. Visit **www.roughguides.com/free-ebook** or scan the **QR code** opposite
2. Enter the code **ireland658**
3. Follow the simple step-by-step instructions

For troubleshooting contact: mail@roughguides.com

Contents

6 Introduction

12 10 Things not to miss

14 A perfect tour of Ireland

16 Wild Atlantic Way

18 Food tour

20 History

33 Places

33 Dublin

46 Dublin day trips

54 The Southeast

64 The Southwest

75 The West

88 The Northwest

90 Northern Ireland

101 **Things to do**
- 101 Outdoor activities
- 104 Shopping
- 108 Culture
- 110 Festivals and events

112 **Food and drink**

125 **Travel essentials**

140 **Index**

Introduction

The grass really does grow greener in Ireland – it's not called the 'Emerald Isle' for nothing. Ireland is a small country, and one to savour slowly. The quick-changing sky adds to the drama of the encounter between land and sea. You're never further than 115km (70 miles) from Ireland's dramatic 4,800-km (3,000-mile) coastline. Far to the west lies America, a beacon for countless emigrants during the nineteenth century. To the east lies Britain, whose relationship with its next-door neighbour has for eight hundred years been one of the most sensitive and dramatic in European geopolitics; the negotiations surrounding Brexit and the so-called 'Irish backstop' providing the latest chapter in this ongoing saga.

The proximity of the Gulf Stream keeps winters in Ireland mild. Snow is rare, rain is not. Significant rainfall is recorded on three out of every four days near the west coast, and on every second day in the east, ranging from stormy torrents to refreshing mists so nebulous that they leave the streets unmarked. Sunshine is rarely far behind, however.

There are, of course, two Irelands – the 26 counties of the Republic and the six counties of Northern Ireland (each with their own government) – and two capitals: Dublin and Belfast. Dublin is a lively city of broad avenues, green parks, and cultural attractions, buzzing with creative energy and a delightfully subversive sense of humour.

NOTES

Almost 7 million people live on the island – fewer than before the Great Famine of the 1840s. Emigration was high until the 'Celtic Tiger' boom, when jobs in new industries kept locals at home. The economy nosedived in 2008, but had recovered its feet by 2016, only for Brexit to unleash another wave of uncertainty. Applications for Irish passports by second-generation Irish living in Britain soared as the UK prepared to leave the EU.

Belfast, historically Ireland's industrial centre, is a little more grounded, but undergoing its own renaissance.

Largely, though, the truly inspiring sights are found outside the big towns. Natural wonders in Ireland can be as awesome as the Cliffs of Moher, or as tranquil as the Lakes of Killarney; as mystical as the holy mountain of Croagh Patrick, or as delightful as the horse-breeding pastures of the Curragh. Scattered amid these natural beauties stand impressive stone relics

Crohy Head Sea Arch

WHAT'S NEW

In Dublin's Trinity College, due to a transformative conservation project, over two hundred thousand volumes have been removed from the Old Library's hallowed shelves. A new exhibition digitally transports visitors into the illuminated pages of the famous Book of Kells manuscript courtesy of two immersive experiences. Two new fantastic museums have opened in other parts of the country: in Limerick, you can see if you've got what it takes to be part of the Irish national team at the **International Rugby Experience**; while County Waterford, saw the opening of the **Irish Wake Museum**, as part of Waterford Treasures. In Belfast, the Titanic Quarter continues to evolve with HMS Caroline now welcoming visitors back on board, and the opening of the Titanic Distillery, the city's first distillery in almost ninety years.

Gorgeous coastline along Slea Head Drive

dating back thousands of years. It was here that remote monastic settlements kept learning alive in Europe during the Dark Ages.

Formerly one of Europe's most conservative corners, with the Catholic Church holding sway in the Republic and fundamentalist Presbyterians powerful in the North, Irish society as a whole has been transformed by progressive politics in the last decade, with divorce, gay marriage and abortion now legal on both sides of the border. Once an island synonymous with emigration, Ireland today welcomes immigrants from around the world.

THE IRISH

More than 1.4 million people live in Dublin, the largest city in the Republic, and home to over a quarter of its population. Belfast, with a metropolitan population of around 645,000, is the hub of Northern Ireland, which remained part of the United Kingdom when the island was partitioned after the Irish War of Independence. Southern Ireland (Éire, latterly the Republic of Ireland), whose birth pangs in 1922 included a civil war, settled down to being a predominantly rural economy, with social affairs and its education system strongly influenced by the Catholic Church.

In the final quarter of the twentieth century, as Northern Ireland was suffering political turmoil, the South transformed itself into a modern European state. A strong youth culture turned Dublin into a party town targeted for weekend breaks by Europe's budget airlines.

The 1998 Good Friday Agreement ushered in a period of peace and prosperity in the North, although ongoing friction between Republicans and Unionists has meant that the devolved government has stopped functioning on several occasions.

WHEN TO GO

Whenever you visit Ireland it's wise to come prepared for wet and/or windy conditions, especially along the west coast, which faces the Atlantic, the source of much of Ireland and Britain's weather. On average it rains around 150 days a year along the east and southeast coasts, and up to as many as 225 days a year in parts of the west and southwest. April is the driest time across most of the island, while December and January are the wettest. Whatever the case, the weather is very changeable and you'll often find a soggy morning rapidly replaced by brilliant sunshine in the afternoon. Most years also see long periods of gorgeous weather, though predicting their occurrence is often well nigh impossible. Generally, the sunniest months are April, May and June, while July and August are the warmest with temperatures sometimes reaching as high as 25°C. Overall, the southeast gets the best of the sunshine.

Belfast City Hall

TALKING IRISH

Centuries of imposed rule from Britain led to the imposition of the English language over Gaelic, which was outlawed. According to the 2016 census, 1.7 million people speak the Irish language, with varying degrees of fluency. Reviving Gaelic – or Irish, as it is usually called – has become state policy; it is taught in schools and printed (along with English) on all official signs and documents. Indeed, in some Gaelic-speaking (Gaeltacht) areas, road signs are in Gaelic only, which can make life difficult for tourists. Irish-medium schools are increasingly popular in both urban and rural Ireland, bringing the Irish language outside of its traditional heartland. Its vocabulary, intonation, and sentence structures have infiltrated the English spoken here, creating great literature and lending everyday speech a touch of poetry.

THE NORTHERN COUNTIES

For the last three decades of the twentieth century, the image of Northern Ireland was tarnished by the violent sectarian conflict, known as 'The Troubles', between Protestant Unionists and Catholic Republicans. Since the Good Friday Agreement was signed in 1998, a more harmonious co-existence prevails, although animosities can still be ignited, particularly around 'marching season' (April–August), while the National Assembly has been suspended on numerous occasions. Brexit also caused uncertainty about future peace prospects but the border remains open and initial fears have calmed. In spite of its turbulent past, residents here are down-to-earth, humorous and friendly, and the scenery is quite spectacular.

SUSTAINABLE TRAVEL

Ireland is reinforcing its environmental commitment by developing initiatives for locals and tourists alike. As Ireland was the EU's first country to impose plastic bag levies, it's no surprise that it introduced the Deposit Return Scheme in 2024 whereby you are charged a small refundable deposit of 15-25 cents, depending on the size of the bottle or can, with return banks in many petrol stations and most supermarkets.

Ireland is working to decrease public transport fares and improve transport links with more services running for longer. There are also a growing number of bicycle lanes in the major cities to encourage more sustainable modes of transport. With multiple ferry ports north and south, it's also easy to take the slower more sustainable route to Ireland by boat, with direct sailings from the UK, Spain and France.

Dublin City Council (dublincity.ie) organises regular clean-up initiatives, like the Autumn Leaf Collection, while nationwide, the National Spring Clean (https://nationalspringclean.org) throughout April and the Clean Coasts (https://cleancoasts.org) programme are just some initiatives you can get involved in. While the idea of 'cleaning' isn't everyone's definition of a holiday, participating in such schemes allows visitors to help maintain the island's beauty and, better yet, cultivate long-lasting friendships with the warm and gregarious locals.

Visit the country's many markets and independent stores to support the local economy and help preserve traditional trades, skills, and crafts. Consider opting for businesses committed to circular living and sustainable practices, like slow-food restaurants or eco-friendly hotels.

10 Things not to miss

1 **GALWAY BAY OYSTERS**
Come here for the finest oysters and try your hand at shucking at the Galway International Oyster and Seafood Festival. See page 73.

2 **DINGLE PENINSULA**
This idyllic area lives up to visitors' romantic notions of Ireland. See page 73.

3 **GLENDALOUGH**
This remote and beautiful mountain valley shelters an atmospheric monastery. See page 53.

4 **BOOK OF KELLS**
Wonder at the ninth-century *Book of Kells*, before wandering through the city-centre campus. See page 37.

5 **BRÚ NA BÓINNE**
This extraordinary ritual landscape is one of the world's most important prehistoric sites. See page 48.

6 **CORK CITY**
The Food Capital of Ireland, the best producers can be found in Cork City's bustling covered market. See page 64.

7 **TITANIC BELFAST**
A fascinating journey through the city's maritime heritage and the story of the ill-fated RMS *Titanic*. See page 94.

8 **WILD ATLANTIC WAY**
This stunning coastal drive covers 2500km from Donegal to Cork. See page 89.

9 **DERRY'S CITY WALLS**
A visit to Derry is incomplete without a stroll around the ramparts. See page 37.

10 **DUBLIN PUBS**
Feel the heartbeat of the city's social life, with over seven hundred venues to choose from. See page 37.

A perfect tour of Ireland

DAY 1

Dublin. Walk the streets of Georgian Dublin, from Trinity College's cobbled quadrangle to the wide expanse of Merrion Square, then enjoy a light lunch at the National Gallery. Cross the Ha'penny Bridge and walk up O'Connell Street to the engaging General Post Office Museum.

DAY 2

Kilkenny and Tipperary. Leave Dublin by car for Kilkenny and head for the Castle, a magnificent edifice in rich parkland beside the River Nore. Have lunch at the Kilkenny Design Centre, an emporium of Irish crafts. Drive on to Tipperary and climb the Rock of Cashel.

DAY 3

Cork City. Explore the city on foot, lunching in the vast covered market. Then take a 20-minute train ride to the port town of Cobh, the last sight of home for generations of emigrants.

DAY 4

Coast path to Killarney. The west Cork coastal road (N71) meanders through villages, where the pubs serve artisan foods. Then it's on to Bantry House, and sub-tropical Glengarriff. Drive through Kenmare to Moll's Gap for a jaw-dropping approach to Killarney.

DAY 5 & 6

Kerry. Explore the beautiful lakes and heather-clad mountains of Killarney. The Gap of Dunloe excursion includes a lake cruise, join it at Ross Castle.

DAY 7

Cliffs of Moher. At Lahinch, you can surf the same Atlantic breakers that pound the nearby Cliffs of Moher. Warm up with Irish stew in Doolin while foot-tapping to live Irish music, and consider a day trip to the Aran Islands, or a visit to the Burren's numerous megalithic remains.

DAY 8

The wild west. Drive west from Galway to Connemara, a sparsely populated wilderness of bog, scattered blue lakes, and distant purple mountains. Enjoy the seafood in Clifden, then head for Connemara National Park. Hike up Diamond Hill for a panoramic view.

DAY 9

The Antrim Coast. Marvel at the Giant's Causeway's basalt columns. Dare to walk the Carrick-A-Rede Rope Bridge before a bite to eat at the Bushmills Inn (see page 96), next door to Ireland's oldest distillery. Nearby are the evocative clifftop ruins of Dunluce Castle.

DAY 10

Belfast. An impressive Victorian city with chic bars and restaurants, compelling museums and quirky libraries. Visit Titanic Belfast, birthplace of the ill-fated liner, then take a walk along the Falls Road to inspect the fascinating murals.

Wild Atlantic Way

DAY 1

Kinsale to Skibbereen. From the handsome heritage town of Kinsale, head south to the Old Head of Kinsale – a little peninsula with great views. Continue west along the R600 to Clonakilty before continuing on to Skibbereen, home to a fantastic heritage centre with a Great Famine commemoration exhibition.

DAY 2

Baltimore to Portmagee. From Skibbereen it's a 20-minute drive to Baltimore, an idyllic village and the perfect place to do a spot of whale-watching: humpback whales, basking sharks, and Risso's dolphins can all be seen here. Have lunch and a pint at *Rolf's* restaurant. Continue to Cahersiveen, a small town overlooking Valentia Harbour; it's worth the steep walk to the summit of Beentee Mountain for the views. End the day in Portmagee, for great pubs and seafood.

DAY 3

The Burren and Cliffs of Moher. Spend the morning exploring the otherworldly Burren landscape, calling into the Burren Nature Sanctuary in Kinvara. From there it's a short drive to the Cliffs of Moher. Whether seen on a clear day or in blustery rain, they are a sight to behold. From here it's 15-minutes to lively Lahinch.

DAY 4

Galway. Head for Galway, vibrant, fun loving and packed with pubs, stop for lunch at *McDonagh's Seafood Bar* for some of the famous local oysters. On into Connemara, your next stop is Clifden, whose spectacular setting is a good spot to pause. County Mayo then beckons, where Westport is your base for the night.

DAY 5

Bogs and Irish art. Head to Ceide Fields, a five thousand-year-old farming community preserved under the bog. Pushing on, pause for an hour at Strandhill, before reaching Sligo Town, whose strong links to Jack.B. Yeats are manifest in the Model gallery. Later, head north to Bundoran's sandy shores.

DAY 6

Slieve League. Head west to the awesome sea cliffs of Slieve League, which include one of the most thrilling cliff scenes in the world, the Amharc Mor. The temptation would be to stay all day but press on to the gorgeously picturesque Glenveagh National Park & Castle before bedding down for the night.

DAY 7

Donegal. The drive around Donegal's Northern Headlands is spectacular. From Buncrana it's a 25-minute drive to Grianán Ailigh, an ancient stone fort on the Inishowen Peninsula. Afterwards, it's on up to Malin Head, the most northerly point in Ireland for a blustery walk around Banba's Crown before returning to Buncrana for the night.

Food tour

DAY 1

Dublin. Where better to start this gastronomic odyssey than the capital. After surveying the magnificent *Book of Kells* at Trinity College, take lunch at *The Fumbally*, before heading west to the Guinness Storehouse, where you can learn all about the legendary drink. Dine in the Michelin one-star *Bastible* on the south side then round off the evening with a pint in the Cobblestone, a magnet for traditional music fans.

DAY 2

Wicklow to Waterford. From Dublin head south to the renowned Ballyknocken House, Farm and Cookery School, where you can learn how to make perfect Irish soda scones and Irish stew using local lamb from the surroundings mountains – which is where you should spend the afternoon walking off lunch. Continue on down to Waterford, dining at *Bodega*, before bedding down for the night.

DAY 3

Cork. Onwards to Cork, but not before a stop off at the country's most celebrated cookery school – Ballymaloe, run by the chef Darina Allen. First, the chefs will demonstrate the techniques used in preparing fish with Irish ingredients, and then it's time for you to put them into practice. Continue after lunch to Cork, which styles itself as the Food Capital of Ireland, and the best producers can be found here in Cork City's bustling covered market; look out for *drisheen*, a type of black pudding.

DAY 4

Kinsale. The southwest's real culinary honeypot is Kinsale, with its beautiful harbour setting. The pick of the crop is the *Fishy Fishy Café and Restaurant*, which does for either lunch or dinner. Take time too, to visit Kinsale's most compelling sight, the formidable Charles Fort.

DAY 5

Clonakilty to Schull. Heading further west, you'll come to the source of the famous Clonakilty Black Pudding, sold at Twomey's butcher's. Enjoy dinner at swish *Inchydoney Island Lodge and Spa*. Continue onto Schull where the Ferguson family produce their excellent Gubbeen cheese and meats. They sell at various local markets, including the Sunday morning Schull Market (Easter to Sept).

DAY 6

Limerick to the Burren. From Schull, head north to Limerick where a brace of fine museums will ensure that you work up an appetite. Take lunch at *House*, overlooking the Quay, before venturing west to the fabulous Burren Smokehouse. Stay the night in Ennis.

DAY 7

Galway. From Ennis, continue north to Galway, which means oysters. Spend the afternoon with a visit to the illuminating Galway City Museum before dinner at *Oscar's Seafood Bistro* for some fishcakes or Galway rock oysters.

History

Stone-Age relics reveal that Ireland has been inhabited since 8,000 BC. The first settlers probably travelled on foot from Scandinavia to Scotland – Britain was once linked to northern Europe by land – then across the narrow sea gap to Ireland.

Stone Age tombs and temples are strewn across the country, from simple stone tripods in farmer's fields to sophisticated passage-graves built on astronomical principles and decorated with mysterious engravings. New settlers introduced Bronze-Age skills from Europe, but the Iron Age arrived in Ireland relatively late.

The Roman legions that rolled across Western Europe into Britain stopped at the Irish Sea and Ireland was left to develop its own way of life during the centuries of the great Roman Empire. Though Irish society comprised scores of oft-feuding mini-kingdoms, a single culture did develop. Druids and poets told legends in a common tongue clearly identifiable as an early form of the Irish language, which later gave rise to Scots Gaelic and Manx.

ST PATRICK'S DAY

The Celts frequently staged raids on Roman Britain for booty and slaves. During one fifth-century sortie, they took a 16-year-old boy named Patrick captive. After spending a few years as a humble shepherd, he escaped to Gaul, became a monk, returned to convert 'the heathens' to Christianity and ultimately became one of Ireland's three patron saint. On this remote, rural and scantly populated island, St Patrick and his successors developed a system of monasteries which kept the flame of Western culture alight while the rest of Europe fumbled through the Dark Ages. Scholarly minds from around Europe converged on the 'island of saints and scholars' to participate in its religious and intellectual life; Irish monks created beautiful, illuminated manuscripts, while others travelled to Britain and mainland Europe, founding monasteries.

THE VIKINGS

At the turn of the ninth century, heavily armed warriors sailed in from Scandinavia aboard sleek boats. The defenceless Irish monasteries, full of relics and treasures, were easy targets. The Vikings' shallow-draught ships moved in quickly and attacked at will, making their way around the Irish coast and up the country's rivers. This danger inspired the building of multi-storey 'round towers', which variously served as watchtowers, belfries, storehouses, and places of refuge (the remains of 65 such towers still stand). The Vikings also established trading colonies around the coast and founded Ireland's first major settlements: Dublin, Waterford and Limerick.

While the Irish learned sailing, weaponry, and metalworking from the Norse, they resented their presence. In the end, the natives ousted the Vikings, with the last clash taking place in 1014 at the Battle of Clontarf, when the High King of Ireland, Brian Ború, defeated the Norse and their Irish allies, although he himself was killed in the battle.

Bronze cast of Vikings Strongbow and Aoife, Waterford

RIVALRY AND REVENGE

Ireland's next invasion was motivated by jealousy. In 1152, the wife of Tiernan O'Rourke, an Irish warrior king, was carried off by rival Dermot MacMurrough of Leinster. Allegedly the lady was a willing victim, possibly even the instigator. O'Rourke got his queen back a few months later and forced Dermot to flee, first to England in 1166, and then France. But from there, Dermot was able to shape an alliance with a powerful Norman nobleman, the Earl of Pembroke. The Earl, known as Strongbow, agreed to lead an army to sweep Dermot back to power. In exchange, the Earl was to be given the hand of Dermot's daughter and the right to succeed him to the Leinster throne. The hardy Normans – the elite of Europe's warrior cultures – won the Battle of Waterford in 1170, and Strongbow married his princess in Waterford's grand cathedral. In further engagements, the Norman war machine stunned, and swiftly defeated Viking and Irish forces. Indeed, things were going so well for Strongbow that his overlord, King Henry II of England, arrived in 1171 to assert his sovereignty.

THE ENGLISH ASCENDANCY

The Anglo-Norman occupation brought profound and long-lasting changes. Towns, churches and castles were built alongside institutions for feudal government. There was much resentment among the Irish, but for the colonial rulers the challenge of revolt was less

BATTLE OF THE BOYNE

Ireland became the battleground for an English power struggle when William of Orange, a Dutch Protestant, challenged his father-in-law (and uncle), the Catholic James II, for the British throne. From exile in France, James sailed to Ireland to mobilise allies and met William's army in July 1690 at the River Boyne. The Orangemen, aided by troops from several Protestant countries, vastly outnumbered the Irish and French forces. The anniversary of William's victory is still celebrated with fervour by Protestants in Northern Ireland.

A pretty Celtic resting place in Glendalough

serious than the danger of total cultural assimilation. With settlers adopting the ways of the natives, rather than the other way round, the Statutes of Kilkenny were introduced in 1366, banning intermarriage and forbidding the English from speaking Gaelic.

English control was consolidated when the House of Tudor turned its attention to Ireland. Henry VIII, the first English monarch to be titled 'King of Ireland', introduced the Reformation to Ireland, but Protestantism took root only in the Pale (the area around Dublin) and in the large provincial towns under English control. In the rest of Ireland, Catholic monasteries carried on as before, as did the Irish language.

From the mid-sixteenth century, the implementation of the so-called plantation policy heralded the large-scale redistribution of wealth. Desirable farmland was confiscated from Catholics

Emigration statue, County Cork

and given to Protestant settlers. During the reign of Elizabeth I, revolts were widespread, but the most unyielding resistance was in the northeastern province of Ulster – Irish chieftains formed an alliance with the Queen's bitter enemy, Spain, and in 1601, a Spanish mini-armada sailed into the southern port of Kinsale. The English defeated the invaders, and many of the Irish earls were exiled to Europe. During the reign of James I, most of the north was confiscated and 'planted' with thousands of Scots and English, who changed the face of the province.

After the English Civil War, Oliver Cromwell ruthlessly massacred the garrisons at Drogheda and Wexford in retribution for their support of Charles I, and pursued his own colonisation of Ireland. From 1654, Cromwell declared that Catholics were only allowed to hold land west of the River Shannon, much of it scarcely habitable. 'To Hell or to Connaught' was the slogan used to sum up the dilemma for the dispossessed, in reference to the province they were allowed to live in.

After the religious war that culminated in the Battle of the Boyne, the Irish Catholic majority was subjected to further persecution in the form of the Penal Laws, introduced by the all-Protestant Irish parliament and designed to keep Catholics away from positions of power and influence.

REVOLUTIONARY IDEAS

It took the American Revolution to inspire daring new thinking in Ireland, with Henry Grattan leading agitation for greater freedom and tolerance. A Protestant of aristocratic heritage, Grattan staunchly defended the rights of all Irishmen in the House of Commons. Further pressure came from an Irish Protestant, Theobald Wolfe Tone, a young lawyer campaigning for parliamentary reform and the abolition of anti-Catholic laws. In 1793 Catholic landholders won the vote and other concessions thanks to Tone. In 1798 a French squadron came to the aid of Tone's United Irishmen off the coast of Cork. It was swiftly intercepted by British naval forces and Wolfe Tone was captured. Convicted of treason, he slit his throat before his sentence of death by hanging could be carried out.

In 1801 the Irish Parliament voted itself out of business by approving the Act of Union, which established the United Kingdom of Great Britain and Ireland. All Irish MPs would now sit at Westminster. In 1823, Daniel O'Connell founded the Catholic Association to work for emancipation. Five years later, he won a seat in the House of Commons, but as a Catholic was legally forbidden to take it. To prevent conflict, Parliament passed the Roman Catholic Relief Act (1829), removing the most discriminatory laws and paving the way for Catholic Emancipation.

NOTES

Daniel O'Connell was one of the first Irish Catholics to qualify as a barrister, and went on to secure the repeal of anti-Catholic legislation in 1829, which earned him the sobriquet 'the Liberator'.

STARVATION AND EMIGRATION

One of the worst disasters of nineteenth-century Europe was the Great Famine. In September 1845, potato blight was found on farms in southeast Ireland. The British government set up an investigation, but the outbreak was misdiagnosed. The next crop failed across Ireland, wiping out the staple food of the Irish peasant. Cruel winter weather and the outbreak of disease added to the horror of starvation. Believing that they should not interfere with free market forces, the British government did not provide relief or intervene.

Survivors fled the stricken land aboard leaking, creaking 'coffin ships'. Irish refugees swamped towns such as Liverpool, Halifax, Boston, and New York. The famine reduced the population of Ireland by over two million – half dying, the rest emigrating. The population has never returned to pre-famine figures, and a pattern of emigration was established – exporting Irish people, politics, culture, traditions, and sport all over the globe.

The remains of the Dublin Bread Company after the Easter Rising

FRUSTRATION AND REVOLT

Towards the end of the nineteenth century, the charismatic leader Charles Stewart Parnell came close to winning Home Rule for Ireland, until it was revealed he was having an affair with a married woman and lost support. Nationalist sentiment and resentment continued to grow, though, and in 1905 a political party called Sinn Féin (translating as 'We Ourselves') was formed. The Home Rule Act was eventually passed by the House of Commons, but the outbreak of World War I placed it on hold.

During the 1916 Easter Rising, nationalist and socialist insurgents seized several strategic buildings, including Dublin's General Post Office, from where they declared Ireland's independence. The authorities crushed the rising, which lacked widespread support (many Irishmen were fighting alongside the British on the Western Front, believing Home Rule would be granted after the war), but their pitiless execution of the ringleaders reversed public opinion. The fight for independence was reinvigorated.

At the next general election Sinn Féin, led by Éamon de Valera, won by a landslide. The newly elected parliamentarians refused to take their seats in London's House of Commons, and instead set themselves up in Dublin as Dáil Éireann, the new parliament of Ireland.

More than two years of guerrilla warfare followed until the Anglo-Irish Treaty was signed by leading IRA General Michael Collins in December 1921, accepting the partition of Ireland. Six counties in the north were allowed to remain part of the United Kingdom. The other 26 counties had a Catholic majority and became the Irish Free State (Éire), a dominion within the British Empire. Many Irish republicans rejected the treaty and a bitter civil war erupted, claiming over 1,000 lives and lasting until 1923. Nine years later Éamon de Valera came to power, vowing to reinstate the ancient Gaelic language and culture. The 26 counties of Éire remained neutral in World War II and formally became an independent republic in 1949.

In Northern Ireland, where Protestants wielded power from Stormont, many Catholics did not recognise the province's legitimacy. The best housing and good jobs in industries such as shipbuilding were almost exclusively the preserve of Protestants, and the Royal Ulster Constabulary was perceived as a sectarian force, breeding huge resentment within impoverished Catholic enclaves. In the late 1960s, civil rights marches against these injustices were violently repressed, unleashing mass rioting. The British Army were sent onto the streets in 1969 and were initially welcomed by the minority Catholic communities. Soon, though, the occupying soldiers were seen as siding with the Unionists, and incidents such as Bloody Sunday, when paratroopers shot 28 unarmed civilians, inflamed the conflict.

After three decades of violence, the Good Friday Agreement, signed in 1998, established a framework for a peaceful, self-governing Northern Ireland. In 2005, the IRA declared a permanent ceasefire and decommissioned its weapons, preparing the way for the formation of a new government in May 2007. British troops

Anti-Brexit protest along Whitehall, London

finally left, and the border between the north and south, so long a livid scar, became almost invisible.

In 2002, Ireland was one of the first twelve countries to adopt the euro. With the creation of new industries and huge investment in infrastructure, the 'Celtic Tiger' roared. Then, in the wake of the 2008 global financial crisis, Ireland entered a severe recession, accepting an €85 billion bailout to survive the international economic crisis. By 2014 it had emerged from the recession, but the Brexit referendum in 2016 was to cast another shadow.

Leo Varadkar

Across Ireland, however, socially progressive politics have blossomed. In a historic 2015 referendum, Ireland voted overwhelmingly in favour of legalizing same-sex marriage, and in 2017, Leo Varadkar, the openly gay son of an Indian immigrant was voted in as Taoiseach. Varadkar's appointment was seen by many commentators as a sign, not only of a generational shift in Irish politics, but also as a transition from conservative traditionalism to liberal modernity. As if to emphasize this fact, in 2018 the country voted by a landslide to legalise abortion. Northern Ireland followed suit a year later. In March 2024, Varadkar announced that he was resigning as Fine Gael leader as well as standing down as Taoiseach, and was replaced by Simon Harris who, at the age of 37, became the youngest Taoiseach in the country's history.

Meanwhile in the north, in 2024 Michelle O'Neill became the country's first nationalist First Minister. And in the UK general election that same year, Sinn Féin became, for the first time, the largest Northern Ireland party in Westminster.

CHRONOLOGY

c.500 BC Celts migrate to Britain. Ireland's Iron Age begins.
c.432 St Patrick converts Ireland to Christianity.
1014 Brian Ború, High King of Ireland, defeats the Vikings.
1366 Statutes of Kilkenny forbid intermarriage or to speak Gaelic.
1541 Henry VIII declares himself King of Ireland.
1690 William of Orange defeats England's Catholic King James II at the Battle of the Boyne.

Simon Harris

1800–01 Act of Union makes Ireland part of the United Kingdom.
1845–49 The Great Famine; over 1 million people die.
1918–23 Sinn Féin forms Irish parliament in Dublin. The 1921 Anglo-Irish Treaty creates the Irish Free State, sparking civil war.
1949 Having remained neutral in World War II, Éire leaves the British Commonwealth and becomes the Republic of Ireland.
1972 British soldiers shoot 28 demonstrators on 'Bloody Sunday', killing 14. Belfast's parliament is dissolved. Northern Ireland is ruled from London.
1973 The Republic of Ireland joins the EEC (now the European Union).
1998 The Good Friday Agreement is signed in Northern Ireland.
2011 After the collapse of the Fianna Fail government, a coalition government is formed by Fine Gael and Labour. Queen Elizabeth II pays her first visit to Ireland.
2015 The Republic of Ireland legalises same-sex marriage.
2016 Britain votes to leave the EU, raising fears that a hard border will be re-established between the Republic and Northern Ireland.
2017 Power-sharing between Unionists and Republicans in NI collapses, leaving the North with no functioning government.
2018 Ireland legalises abortion. Michael D. Higgins re-elected President.
2019 Abortion is decriminalised and same-sex marriage is legalised in Northern Ireland
2020 Ireland goes into lockdown to stop the spread of Covid-19. A coalition government between Fine Gael, Fianna Fáil and the Green Party is formed.
2021 Lockdown ends in May and tourists are welcomed back into the country.
2022 Northern Ireland assembly suspended for a sixth time.
2024 Leo Varadkar resigns. Simon Harris takes over, age 37. Michelle O'Neill becomes Northern Ireland's first nationalist First Minister. General election results in a coalition government.

Dublin's Samuel Beckett Bridge

Places

The best way to see Ireland is by car, though various package deals or bus tours exist as an alternative. You can see a good deal of the country using public transport, although apart from the main routes, the bus schedules are designed more for locals than tourists.

This book covers the highlights of the Republic and Northern Ireland, starting in Dublin and proceeding clockwise. We cannot describe all the sights – or all the counties – but wherever you go, you'll enjoy Ireland best at an unhurried Irish pace.

DUBLIN

HIGHLIGHTS

- O'Connell Street to St Stephen's Green, see page 34
- Medieval Dublin, see page 40
- The North Bank, see page 42
- Beyond the Centre, see page 45

The Republic of Ireland's capital (circa 1.4 million) is the birthplace and muse of many great authors, and an elegant European city with many outstanding examples of eighteenth-century architecture. A vibrant, dynamic place, **Dublin** ❶ remains utterly beguiling and an essential part of any visit to the country. Alongside the city's historic buildings – its cathedrals and churches, Georgian squares and townhouses, castles, monuments and pubs, you'll discover grand new hotels and shopping centres, stunning new street architecture and a state-of-the-art tramway system.

NOTES

The city's name comes from the Irish 'Dubh Linn', meaning 'a dark pool'. The alternative Gaelic name, 'Baile Átha Cliath', means 'the town of the hurdle ford'.

WHERE TO SHOOT THE BEST PICTURES

Banks of the Liffey, Dublin Photograph Custom House from the banks of the River Liffey and capture this magnificent neoclassical building in all its glory, set against the tranquil waters of the river.
Glendalough, Wicklow Shoot the eleventh-century round tower, the ninth-century barrel-vaulted church known as St Kevin's Kitchen', and the roofless cathedral.
St Fin Barr's Cathedral, Cork From the opposite side of the square out front, point your viewfinder at the spire-studded skyline to capture the cathedral in the cityscape.
The Conor Pass, Kerry This mountaineous road has breathtaking scenery, Stop along the route where there are allocated parking places and snap away.
Skellig Michael, Kerry The island is great for landscape photos and during the breeding season also for bird photography. Get a shot of the abandoned monastery with its iconic beehive huts.
The Burren, Clare The otherworldly, moonscape landscape of the Burren will always remind you of your trip to Ireland.
Queen's University, Belfast The stunning Lanyon Building is the most iconic and makes for the best photographs.

O'CONNELL STREET TO ST STEPHEN'S GREEN

The main avenue in Dublin is O'Connell Street. Measuring 46m (150ft) across, it has several monuments to Irish history lined along the middle, none more spectacular than The **Dublin Spire**, a 395-foot high stainless-steel monument which replaced the nineteenth-century Nelson's Pillar blown up by anti-British rebels in 1966.

O'Connell Street's most famous landmark is the General Post Office (GPO), which served as the insurgents' headquarters during the 1916 Easter Rising and was badly damaged in the fighting. The state-of-the-art **GPO Museum** (charge; www.gpowitnesshistory.ie) explores the conflict, as well as its causes and aftermath, through slick touchscreens, audiovisual booths and many previously unseen artefacts.

Just opposite O'Connell Bridge is the imposing monument honouring 'The Liberator', Daniel O'Connell (1775–1847, see page 25), after whom both the street and bridge are named.

From the bridge, wider than it is long, you can look along the embankments of the River Liffey. To the east rises the copper dome of the eighteenth-century **Custom House** (charge; www.heritage ireland.ie), which, like many buildings along the Liffey, was badly damaged in the Irish War of Independence (1919–21) and subsequent Civil War (1922–23); inside, a fabulous new exhibition has interactive screens and virtual displays in each room focusing on an architectural aspect of the building or some historical element. To the west is the Ha'penny Bridge, so-called because that's what it originally cost to cross.

The General Post Office

The imposing white building facing College Green on the south side of the River Liffey is a branch of the **Bank of Ireland**, originally home of the Irish parliament in the eighteenth century. The bank moved in when parliament was abolished by the Act of Union in 1801 (see page 25).

Across the road stands **Trinity College** Ⓐ founded by Queen Elizabeth I in 1592 and a timeless enclave of calm and scholarship in the middle of this bustling city. Until 1793 it was an exclusively Protestant institution, and the Catholic Church forbade Catholics to attend Trinity 'under pain of mortal sin' right up until the late 1960s. Today, TCD, as it is called, is integrated. The campus forms a beautiful monument to academia and architecture, and visitors can enjoy cobbled walks among trimmed lawns, fine old trees, statues, and stone buildings. From just inside the main gates, Trinity students lead entertaining forty-five-minute **walking tours** of the college (mid-May to Aug 3–4 daily).

Fellows Square and the Old Library at Trinity College

The greatest treasures are in the vaulted Long Room in the **Old Library** (charge; www.visittrinity.ie), where double-decker shelving holds thousands of books published prior to 1800, and priceless early manuscripts are displayed in glass cases. In the adjacent Colonnades Gallery, queues of tourists reverently wait for a look at

TEMPLE BAR

Temple Bar is a network of small streets full of studios, galleries, second-hand bookshops, clothing outlets, and music stores, not to mention countless restaurants and pubs. Many Dubliners regard it as a tourist trap, but it has some worthwhile cultural centres.

Project Arts Centre: theatre and avant-garde art gallery.
The Button Factory: nightclub and concert venue.
Irish Film Institute: arthouse cinema with bookshop, café/restaurant, bar, and film archive.
Photo Museum Ireland: exhibits Irish and international work.
National Photographic Archive: maintains and exhibits historical images of Ireland.
Jam Art Factory: Irish art and design shop.
The Ark: arts and entertainment centre for children.

the **Book of Kells**. This 340-page parchment wonder, handwritten and illustrated by monks during the ninth century, contains a Latin version of the New Testament. The beauty of the script – the illumination (the decoration of initial letters and words) – and the bright abstract designs make this the most wonderful treasure to survive from Ireland's Golden Age. The vellum leaves are turned every day to protect them from light and to give visitors a chance to come back for more. The library is closing at the end of 2025 to undergo a major conservation project, but in the meantime, a new exhibition digitally transports visitors into the illuminated pages of the famous manuscript courtesy of two immersive experiences in a specially constructed pavilion adjacent to the Museum Building. You can also enjoy art exhibitions at the **Douglas Hyde Gallery**, (www.douglashydegallery.com) and the child-friendly **Science Gallery** (https://dublin.sciencegallery.com).

A left turn on leaving Trinity by the main gate brings you to the beginning of **Grafton Street** ❽, the main shopping and social artery of the city's southside. More than anywhere else, Grafton

Street demonstrates Dublin's knack for seeming to bustle and dawdle at the same time. Buskers entertain passers-by on their way to Brown Thomas, the city's famous high-end department store, and other shopping emporiums, such as the stunning Powerscourt Townhouse Centre, and the Stephen's Green Shopping Centre at the south end. The streets shooting off Grafton St are filled with boutique shops, chain stores and pleasant places to eat (and drink).

Examples of Europe's finest Georgian houses can be seen facing Merrion Square. The discreet, smart brick houses have Georgian doorways flanked by tall columns and topped by fanlights. No two are alike. In a complex of formal buildings on the west side of the square stands the city's largest eighteenth-century mansion, Leinster House, once home to the dukes of Leinster. Today, **Leinster House** is

Christ Church Cathedral

the seat of the Irish parliament, which consists of the Senate *(Seanad Éireann)* and the Chamber of Deputies (the *Dáil*, pronounced 'doyle'). Just north of here, on Merrion Square West, is the **National Gallery of Ireland** Ⓒ (permanent collection free, charge for some exhibitions; www.nationalgallery.ie). Outside you will see a statue of George Bernard Shaw, the famous and respected Dubliner known locally as a benefactor of the institution. The gallery has a collection of over 16,300 artworks. Irish artists receive priority, not least an entire room given over to Jack B. Yeats (1871–1957), but other nationalities are well represented, such as Dutch, English, Flemish, French, Italian, and Spanish masters, including Fra Angelico, Rubens, Rembrandt, Canaletto, Gainsborough, Goya, Van Gogh, and Renoir.

The main entrance to the **National Museum of Ireland** Ⓓ (free; www.museum.ie), a Dublin institution showcasing the country's archaeology and history, is reached from Kildare Street. Its collection of antiquities holds several surprises, from Irish bog bodies to exquisite gold ornaments of the Bronze Age. Famous items include the eight-century Ardagh Chalice, the delicate Tara Brooch from the same era and the twelfth-century Shrine of St Patrick's Bell. You can also see ancient Ogham stones and replicas of the greatest carved stone crosses from the early centuries of Christian Ireland.

Dublin is well-endowed with squares and parks, including **St Stephen's Green** Ⓔ one of the biggest city squares in Europe. During the eighteenth century the square was almost completely surrounded by elegant town houses, some of which survive today, Inside the square is a delightful park with flower gardens and an artificial lake favoured by waterfowl. Among many sculptures and monuments is a memorial to the poet and playwright W.B. Yeats by Henry Moore, a bust of James Joyce, and another of Constance Markiewicz, who defended the square during the 1916 insurrection, and who was the first woman elected to the British House of Commons. (She declined to take her seat, in line with Sinn Féin's abstentionist policy, but served in the Dáil after Independence.)

Another statue honours the man who paid for landscaping the square: Lord Ardilaun, son of the founder of the Guinness brewery. Some thirsty sightseers might be inspired to find a nearby pub and raise a toast to this stout-hearted benefactor.

MEDIEVAL DUBLIN

Dublin Castle F (charge; www.dublincastle.ie), set on a hill above the original Viking settlement on the south bank of the River Liffey, dates to the thirteenth century, but was mostly rebuilt during the eighteenth century. Over the years it has served as a seat of government, a prison, a courthouse, and occasionally as a fortress under siege. Guided tours take in the grand State Apartments, as well as the **Chapel Royal** in the Lower Yard, an ornate Gothic Revival gem built in 1814 but now deconsecrated, and the excavations of the **Undercroft**. Just behind the castle is the **Chester Beatty Library** G (free; www.chesterbeatty.ie), home to a collection of priceless manuscripts and miniatures: jade books from China, early Arabic tomes on geography and astronomy, a sampling of Korans, and rare Gospel texts. Around the corner from the castle stands City Hall, built in the late eighteenth century in solid, classical style. Downstairs, an exhibition tells the story of the Irish capital.

Dublin has two noteworthy cathedrals, and although it is the official capital of what is a predominantly Catholic country, both belong to the Protestant Church of Ireland.

Christ Church Cathedral H (charge; http://christchurchcathedral.ie) is the older of the two, dating from 1038. One unusual architectural touch is the covered pedestrian bridge over Winetavern Street, which links the church and its Synod Hall; this was built during the Victorian era, but doesn't spoil the overall mood. Otherwise, the cathedral contains Romanesque, Early English, and fine neo-Gothic elements.

The crypt, now displaying many of Christ Church's valuable treasures, runs under the length of the church, and is a surviving remnant from the twelfth century, during which time the cathedral was expanded by Strongbow (see page 22), whose remains reputedly lie buried here, although there is some debate about the authenticity of the Strongbow tomb. You can see the fine statue of a recumbent cross-legged knight in full armour upstairs.

If you would like to delve deeper into Viking and medieval Dublin visit the Synod Hall to see an impressive living history museum Dublinia (charge; www.dublinia.ie). Actors recreate how Viking and medieval Dubliners lived and encourage visitors to get involved too. Great for kids of all ages.

A short walk south from Christ Church Cathedral leads to Dublin's slightly newer and larger cathedral, **St Patrick's** ❶ (charge; www.stpatrickscathedral.ie), which is dedicated to Ireland's national saint.

A classic Irish pub in Temple Bar

It is said that St Patrick himself baptised fifth-century converts at a well on this very site; indeed, a stone slab used for covering the well can be found in the northwest of the cathedral. This church was consecrated in 1192, but the present structure dates mostly from the thirteenth and fourteenth centuries. The cathedral is known for its association with Jonathan Swift, author of *Gulliver's Travels*, who was appointed dean in 1713 and served until his death in 1745. Many Swiftian relics occupy a corner of the north transept, and a simple brass plate in the floor near the entrance marks his grave; next to this you can see the tomb of his beloved 'Stella'. Above the lintel of the robing room you can read his self-written epitaph, etched in Latin on Kilkenny marble: 'Here lies the body of Jonathan Swift, Doctor of Divinity and Dean of this Cathedral, Where savage indignation can no longer lacerate his heart; Go traveller and imitate if you can, this dedicated and earnest champion of liberty.'

The talented choirboys of St Patrick's Cathedral sing at the services given every day of the week except Saturdays. A joint choir formed from both cathedrals was the first to sing Handel's *Messiah* when the composer was in Dublin in 1742. A copy from the year 1799 can be seen in **Marsh's Library** J (charge; www.marshlibrary.ie), Ireland's first public library, founded in 1701.

Called the 'Left Bank' by tourist officials, **Temple Bar** K (see page 37) is Dublin's cultural quarter, running from Westmoreland Street to Christ Church Cathedral. With its eighteenth- and nineteenth-century architecture it's not just the cultural quarter of Dublin, but also a land of themed bars and raucous nightclubs. It's best on Saturdays as there is a gourmet food market on Meeting House Square, a book market on Temple Bar Square, and a craft and design market on Cow's Lane.

THE NORTH BANK

The most impressive building located on the north bank of the Liffey is the domed Four Courts (originally the Chancery, Common

Pleas, Exchequer and King's Bench). This is the magnificent work of James Gandon, the respected eighteenth-century English-born architect, who also designed Dublin's Custom House. The courthouse was seriously damaged by prolonged shelling during the 1922–23 civil war, but after lengthy reconstruction it was fully restored and justice continues to be dispensed in the Four Courts.

St Michan's Church (charge for crypt tours; http://cathedralgroupdublin.ie) is just around the corner in Church Street. Founded in 1095, it has been rebuilt several times. Among the curiosities is an unusual 'Penitent's Pew', in which sinners had to sit and confess their sins aloud to the whole congregation. In the crypt, wood coffins and mummies can be seen in a remarkable state of preservation – some of which are about eight hundred years' old. You can touch the finger of the mummified crusader for good luck.

The last imposing official building to be designed by the architect James Gandon was the **King's Inns** Ⓛ, which houses the headquarters of the Irish legal profession. It contains an important law library and a magnificent dining hall, where grand portraits of many judges decorate the walls.

On the north side of Parnell Square is Charlemont House, an attractive eighteenth-century mansion that's now the site of

The Four Courts

The Hugh Lane Gallery Ⓜ (free; www.hughlane.ie). It includes works from the fine collection of Sir Hugh Lane, who amassed a considerable collection including works by Renoir, Monet and Degas, as well as Pissarro and the Irish painters Jack B. Yeats, Roderic O'Connor and Louis le Brocquy. The gallery also houses a re-creation of Dublin-born painter **Francis Bacon's studio**, transported from its original location at Reece Mews in South Kensington, London, along with displays of the famous artist's works.

Not far away, at 35 North Great George's Street is the **James Joyce Centre** Ⓝ (charge; www.jamesjoyce.ie) which celebrates the work of perhaps Ireland's most imaginative yet most complex writer.

The Drawing Room in Malahide Castle

BEYOND THE CENTRE

Within easy reach of central Dublin, Phoenix Park (www.phoenixpark.ie) provides Dubliners with nearly 3sq miles (8sq km) of beautiful parkland. Europe's largest urban walled park, it's an ideal place to escape the city's bustle, a popular venue for sports, and offers plenty of spots for a picnic. By the park's Parkgate Street entrance lies the **People's Garden**, a pleasant area of formal flowerbeds and hedges, while the nearby **Wellington Monument** took some 44 years to complete before it was finally unveiled in 1861.

At the park's centre on Chesterfield Avenue rises the **Phoenix Monument**, northwest of which is the **Phoenix Park Visitor Centre** (free), which recounts the history of the park through the ages. On the northeast side of the park, **Dublin** Zoo (charge; www.dublinzoo.ie) – one of Europe's oldest – focuses on raising species threatened by extinction, such as Asian elephants, Amur tigers and waldrapp ibis. Nearby **Farmleigh House** (charge; www.farmleigh.ie) is a 78-acre (31-hectare) estate with a stately home and beautiful gardens that once belonged to the Guinness family.

In **Kilmainham**, a stone tower gate guards the grounds of the Royal Hospital, a former home for army pensioners, but which now holds the **Irish Museum of Modern Art** (free; www.imma.ie). All shows here are temporary and range from retrospectives of major international artists to new works by modern Irish painters and sculptors.

NOTES

The overwhelming demand to see Newgrange during the winter solstice has forced Irish Heritage to hold a lottery. Visitors can sign up in the welcome centre. Or you can email your postal address and contact phone number to brunaboinne@opw.ie and they'll enter your name. From an average 35,000 entries, fifty names are chosen.

The forbidding Kilmainham Gaol (entry by guided tour only, book in advance: charge; www.kilmainhamgaolmuseum.ie) became the place of incarceration for captured revolutionaries, including the leaders of the 1916 Easter Rising. Now carefully restored, guided **tours** provide a chilling impression of the prisoners' living conditions and spartan regime.

Many make their way to the city's biggest commercial enterprise, the Guinness Brewery, situated at St James' Gate since 1759. Its dark, full-bodied stout is world-renowned, and visitors to the seven-storey **Guinness Storehouse** (charge; www.guinness-storehouse.com) get an entertaining explanation of how the brew is made and, naturally, a sample of the finished product at the end of the tour. The Gravity Bar at the top of hte building also pleases visitors with superb city views.

DUBLIN DAY TRIPS

HIGHLIGHTS

- North of Dublin, see page 46
- West of Dublin, see page 50
- South of Dublin, see page 52

NORTH OF DUBLIN

The northeastern part of Dublin Bay, Howth peninsula, makes an appealing starting point for those wishing to venture out of Dublin. From the vantage point of the 170-m (560-ft) Hill of Howth, you can survey the bay and the sea. Howth Harbour, on the north side of the peninsula, is a fishing port and departure point for cruises to Ireland's Eye (www.howthcliffcruises.ie), an islet 1.5km (1 mile) offshore that is popular with birds and bird-watchers.

Malahide, a small resort town, is best known for its **castle** (charge; www.malahidecastleandgardens.ie), a two-turreted medieval pile that was home to the Talbot family for more than eight hundred years, until the last surviving member of the family died in 1973. Guided **tours** take in the castle's principal rooms – the Great Hall and Oak Room are the most impressive – while an interactive exhibition in the visitor centre explores the fascinating history of the Talbot Family. The ornamental walled **gardens** are also worth exploring, and are home to the Republic's only butterfly house.

Drogheda ❷, a small industrial town, straddles the River Boyne near the site of the 1690 battle in which King James II failed to recover the British crown (see page 22). This medieval city was surrounded by a wall with 10 gates – you can still drive through the thirteenth-century **St Lawrence's Gate**, with its two towers. In the town centre **St Peter's Church** has been dedicated to St Oliver Plunkett (1628–81), the Archbishop of Armagh who was executed by the British for an alleged papist plot. Several relics of the local saint are displayed in the church, including the actual door of his cell at Newgate Prison and, most amazing of all, his head, which is embalmed and kept in a gold case in a side altar.

About 10km (6 miles) to the northwest is Monasterboice (St Buite's Abbey), one of Ireland's

An early Christian high cross at Monasterboice

numerous ancient monastic settlements. Over it stands the jagged top of what is thought to have been the tallest round tower in Ireland, 34m (110ft) high. Along with the remains of two ruined churches there are three important examples of early Christian high crosses, with intricately carved figures.

Set in peaceful and verdant country, a high medieval gatehouse guards the approach to **Old Mellifont Abbey** (www.mellifont abbey.ie), Ireland's most important early Cistercian monastery. Among the buildings stand the remains of a large church and the Lavabo, a graceful octagonal building of which only four sides remain.

Newgrange ❸ (Brú na Boinne Visitor Centre; charge; www.newgrange.com/www.heritageireland.ie), a large Neolithic tomb

The Neolithic tomb at Newgrange

in the Boyne Valley, looks like a man-made hilltop, but is in fact an amazing feat of prehistoric engineering – one of Europe's best examples of a passage grave. The narrow tunnel leading to the central shrine is positioned to let the sun shine in on the shortest day of the year, 21 December. The 19-m (62-ft) tunnel is just high and wide enough to walk through at a crouch. At its end you can stand in the circular vault and look up at the ceiling to see the remarkable four thousand-year-old technique used in its construction.

NOTES

The ruins of an ancient monastery are at the southern end of County Kildare, in the village of Castledermot. Two beautifully carved crosses remain near the portal of a church that could be as much as one thousand years old. The design of this ruin is repeated in a new church just a few yards behind it.

Carvings in spiral, circular and diamond designs decorate the stones in the inner sanctum and entrance. Outside, a dozen large, upright stones, about a third the original number, form a protective circle. Access is by guided tour only; numbers are limited, so pre-book (last tours 90 min before closing). There are two more Neolithic tumuli at Knowth and Dowth.

A town of unique historical and cultural significance Kells in County Meath, is best known for **Kells Abbey**, a former monastery from which the *Book of Kells* takes its name (see page 36). Today the monastic site includes a 27m **round tower**, **St Colmcilles church** and four stunning **high crosses**. A fifth high cross dating from the ninth century, known as the "market cross", can be found in front of the old courthouse at the east end of town.

As its name indicates, **Trim** ❹ is a well-kept, tidy town, but the English name is derived from the Irish *Baile Átha Trium*, which means 'the town of the Elder Tree Ford'. Trim claims it has Ireland's largest medieval **castle** (charge; www.heritageireland.ie), once a

Norman stronghold. Vast it is, but time has left only the bare bones. Across the river, the Yellow Steeple was part of an Augustinian abbey established in the thirteenth century; the tower was blown up to keep it out of Cromwell's hands.

WEST OF DUBLIN

With some of the greenest pastures in all of Ireland, **County Kildare** is a great area for sports, and there are plenty of historic sites amid the rolling hills. Maynooth, a pleasant town with an historic college and the ruins of a twelfth-century castle, was renowned in the nineteenth and twentieth centuries as a training centre for priests. Founded in 1795 and once one of the foremost Catholic seminaries in the world, **St Patrick's College** is now part of the National University of Ireland.

Powerscourt waterfall

On the edge of Celbridge village, **Castletown House** ❺ (charge; www.castletownhouse.ie) stands at the end of a long avenue of trees. This vast stately home, in Palladian style, was erected in 1722 for the speaker of the Irish House of Commons, William Conolly, and has been restored and refurnished with eighteenth-century antiques and paintings. Conolly's widow ordered the construction of a monstrous obelisk 5km (3 miles) from the house; known as Conolly's Folly, it

THE WICKLOW WAY

You'll need the better part of a week to see all the Wicklow Way, an ancient path stretching 127km (79 miles) from the suburbs of Dublin to the Wexford border town of Clonegal. A shorter option is the popular stretch from Knockree, 5km (3 miles) west of Enniskerry, to Glendalough. It'll take you about three days to cover this area, and you'll be able to step foot on the highest point of the trail – White Hill, from which on a clear day you can see the mountains in Wales.

was erected to provide jobs for local workers suffering from the famine of 1740–41.

The administrative centre of the county, Naas (the Irish *Nás na Ríogh* means 'Assembly Place of the Kings') has an important racecourse. So does nearby Punchestown, but the capital of horse racing and breeding is the **Curragh** ❻, a 2,000 hectare stretch of flat racing turf, grazed by sheep and used for exercise gallops by many training stables. It's a shock to come upon a modern grandstand – site of the Irish Derby – in the middle of this vast plain.

Many winners of the biggest races are born near Kildare Town at the Irish National Stud (charge; www.irishnationalstud.ie), where thoroughbreds live in a first-class 'horse resort'. Aside from seeing the horses, the highlight of a visit here is the Irish Racehorse Experience, a state of the art experiential attraction, whereby visitors can immerse themselves in the life of a thoroughbred horse. The grounds also contain the beautiful **Japanese Garden** – once a bog, now a world of miniature hills and waterfalls, colourful flowers and trees.

The town of **Kildare** is also remembered for the double monastery (monks and nuns) founded there by fifth-century St Brigid. Though Vikings and other invaders damaged the buildings quite badly, the shape of the nineteenth-century **cathedral** features thirteenth-century elements. Nearby is an ancient round tower still in very good shape, with stairs all the way to the top. Another attraction is Kildare Village (daily 10am–8pm; www.thebicester collection.com) for chic outlet shopping.

SOUTH OF DUBLIN

Dún Laoghaire ❼ (pronounced Dunleary), just south of Dublin, a former international port, is Ireland's leading yachting centre, with several clubs located here. Construction of the harbour – whose piers are 2km (1 mile) long – was a great feat of nineteenth-century engineering, and remains impressive. The newest addition to the Dún Laoghaire skyline is the ship prow–like Lexicon Library and Cultural Centre (http://libraries.dlrcoco.ie), with fine views of Dublin Bay from the top floor, situated a few short steps from the National Maritime Museum (charge; www.mariner.ie).

Around 1.5km (1 mile) south at Sandycove is an eighteenth-century Martello tower, built as part of Dublin's coastal defences designed to keep Napoleon at bay. James Joyce stayed here, and the tower features in the opening of his novel *Ulysses*. It now houses the James Joyce Tower and Museum (free; www.joyce-tower.ie), displaying Joyce's guitar, waistcoat and walking stick, as well as one of two official death masks. There are also copious letters, photos, and rare and first editions, notably one of *Ulysses* beautifully illustrated by Matisse.

Just across the border in County Wicklow, the 'Garden of Ireland', the popular resort of Bray (www.bray.ie) has a 2km (1 mile) sand-and-shingle beach backed by an esplanade. The 7km-Cliff Walk along the Bray Head headland leads to Greystones, a postcard-pretty coastal town.

West of Bray, near Enniskerry, is the grand estate of **Powerscourt** ❽ (charge; www.powerscourt.com). Covering 20 hectares (47 acres) of glorious countryside and gardens, the estate has an eighteenth-century, 100-room mansion at its centre, which was damaged in a fire in 1974. From the house, the terraced **Italian**

Gardens slope gracefully down to a grand staircase, which in turn leads down to a spirited pair of zinc-winged horses guarding the **Triton Lake**. The estate's final attraction, **Powerscourt Waterfall**, is Ireland's highest at 120m, but can only be accessed by car.

In a narrow, wooded valley with two lakes stand the evocative ruins of the ancient monastic settlement of **Glendalough** ❾ (www.glendalough.ie). The hermit St Kevin founded the monastery here in the sixth century, evidently inspired by the breathtaking, remote scenery. He planned it as a small, contemplative institution, but as its fame spread far and wide, Glendalough of the Seven Churches became an important monastic centre, until 1398, when it was destroyed by Anglo-Normans.

The surviving buildings date from the eighth and twelfth centuries, the most famous of which is the **round tower**, 34m (112ft) high and 16m (52ft) in circumference at the base. This was the place to sit out any sieges; its doorway is built 3.5m (11ft) above the ground – enough to discourage even Vikings from invading. Remnants of a cathedral, stone churches, and decorated crosses can also be seen, and the original gateway to the settlement, the only one of its kind in Ireland, is still standing. Inside, on the right, a cross-inscribed stone may

Re-enactments at the Irish National Heritage Park

have marked the limit of the sanctuary granted to those who took refuge within the monastery. In the graveyard, tombstones dating back hundreds of years sit next to more recent graves.

Near Rathdrum village, is **Avondale House** (charge; www.beyondthetreesavondale.com), the one-time home of the great nineteenth-century Irish leader, Charles Stewart Parnell; guided tours take in six of the ground floor rooms, which hold numerous, authentic pieces of furniture and artefacts, Recent redevelopment of the estate has incorporated Ireland's first Treetop Walk and Viewing Tower. Russborough House (charge; www.russborough.ie), near Blessington, is an eighteenth-century Palladian mansion, reputed to be the longest house in Ireland at 210m (700ft). It houses a wonderful collection of art and antiques, including works by Goya, Gainsborough, and Reynolds, while the extensive grounds are the location for the **National Bird of Prey Centre** (www.nationalbirdofpreycentre.ie) where you can handle several owl species.

NOTES

In the ninth century Wexford was called *Waesfjord*, meaning 'the harbour of the mudflats'. At low tide, when the bay empties like a sink, the original name still seems appropriate.

THE SOUTHEAST

HIGHLIGHTS

- Wexford, see page 55
- Waterford, see page 57
- Cashel, see page 60
- Kilkenny, see page 61

Over the whole year, the southeast enjoys up to an hour more sunshine a day than other parts of Ireland – perfect for seeing and enjoying the region's magical mountains, pastures, rivers, beautiful beaches, and delightful old towns.

Enniscorthy (the Irish *Inis Coirthe* means Rock Island) is a colourful inland port on the River Slaney, which is navigable from here to Wexford. High above the steep streets of the town, Vinegar Hill is a good vantage point for viewing the countryside. It was the scene of the last battle of the 1798 United Irishmen Rebellion, during which British General Lake overwhelmed the Wexford rebels armed with pitchforks and pikes. **Enniscorthy Castle** (charge; www.enniscorthycastle.ie), in the centre of town, is an imposing Norman keep, rebuilt during the sixteenth century. Now completely renovated, it numbers among its exhibitions a first floor that's been recreated as it might have been when it was last inhabited, in the early twentieth century.

WEXFORD

Wexford, the county seat, 24km (15 miles) south of Enniscorthy, was one of the first Viking settlements in Ireland – a few ancient monuments survive and are well signposted, with informative plaques explaining local legends. The town is more well known for its prestigious Opera Festival (www.wexfordopera.com) in October which attracts performers and fans from around the world.

The **Irish National Heritage Park** ⑩ (charge;

Waterford crystal in the making

Cahir Castle

www.irishheritage.ie) in Ferrycarrig, north of the town, contains a collection of life-size replicas of ancient dwellings, burial sites, old monastic settlements and fortifications, from early Irish man to the twelfth century. **Johnstown Castle** (charge; www.johnstown castle.ie) is a nineteenth-century Gothic Revival mansion whose extensive grounds feature an abundance of trees and plants, outdoors and in hothouses, as well as ornamental lakes, rich woodland, a sunken Italian garden and a ruined medieval tower house. The estate's old farm buildings are now home to the **Irish Agricultural Museum**, which explores rural history via artefacts, a wealth of furniture and machinery, and re-created workshops and kitchens.

Southeast of the town, the resort of Rosslare has a 10km- (6 mile-) a massive and popular sandy beach, while nearby Rosslare

Europort sees car ferries arrive from and depart for destinations in Wales, France and Spain.

The tip of the Hook peninsula is crowned by the 800-year-old Hook Lighthouse (charge for tours; http://hookheritage.ie) – the world's oldest operational lighthouse – where a warning light has been kept burning at Hook Head for the past 1,500 years. For fans of the supernatural (or not), a visit to scenic **Duncannon Fort** (charge; http://duncannonfort.ie), with its purported sightings of a soldier ghost, is a must.

The Norse established ports in Dublin and Wexford, but it somehow never occurred to them to found permanent settlements inland. It was the Normans who moved 32km (20 miles) up the estuary to build **New Ross ⓫**, a sizeable town and still an important inland port. By the riverbank, you will see the tall masts of the Dunbrody Famine Ship (charge; www.dunbrody.com), a full-scale replica of a sailing ship built in 1845 to transport emigrants to North America.

The isolated hamlet of Dunganstown, near New Ross, was the birthplace of US President John F. Kennedy's great grandfather. The **Kennedy Homestead** (charge; www.kennedyhomestead.ie) describes his emigration to the US, fleeing the Famine in 1848, and traces the family's subsequent history. Funded by Irish-Americans in memory of the former US president, who returned to visit his ancestors' homeland in 1963, the John F. Kennedy Arboretum (charge; www.heritageireland.ie) houses an astonishing assortment of more than 4500 trees and shrubs from the world's temperate regions.

WATERFORD

Waterford ⓬ is a largely Georgian port, 29km (18 miles) from the open sea, and from the far side of the River Suir, its long quayside presents a pretty image. Founded in the ninth century, the town did not gain a charter until 1205, granted by King John. The city's most venerable building is **Reginald's Tower** (charge; www.waterfordtreasures.com), a giant circular fortification, 3m- (10ft-)

thick and about 24m- (80ft-) tall, which has survived many sieges since being erected in 1003. It is part of the Waterford Treasures collection of museums which include Bishop's Palace, the Medieval Museum, the Irish Museum of Time, King of the Viking's VR experience, The Silver Museum and the The Wake Museum.

Among other attractions are the Garter Lane Arts Centre (www.garterlane.ie), a lively venue in a converted town house; the Mall, an elegant Georgian street beginning at the Quay; and Waterford City Hall, built in the 1780s, which has many fine features, including two small theatres and a Council Chamber illuminated by a splendid chandelier made from the famous **Waterford crystal**.

Waterford crystal was founded in 1783 but moved into a gleaming new shop and factory on The Mall some time ago. At the **House**

Holy Cross Abbey, Tipperary

of Waterford (charge; www.waterfordvisitorcentre.com), you can join a tour of the factory and watch the making of the beech and pearwood moulds that only last a week, and crystal being cut with diamond-tipped wheels. However, the highlight has to be the heat and noise of the blowing room with its 1300°c furnace, where the red-hot molten crystal is shaped with supreme skill.

In **Lismore** ⓭, at the western edge of the county, the **Lismore Castle Experience** (charge; www.discoverlismore.com), another educational multimedia show tells the history of this small town founded in the seventh century by St Carthage. Also, Ormond Castle in Carrick-on-Suir, Co Tipperary, is the finest Elizabethan manor house in Ireland, now restored to its sixteenth-century glory.

Counties **Kilkenny** and **Tipperary** both feature stunning scenery and imposing ruins: the former entered history as the ancient Kingdom of Ossory, while the latter was home of the kings of Munster. The main town in County Tipperary is Clonmel, where parts of the fourteenth-century walls can still be seen; the turreted West Gate was rebuilt in 1831 on the site of an original gate. The Tipperary **Museum of Hidden History** (charge; www.waterfordvisitorcentre.com) on Mick Delahunty Square brings the town's history vividly to life.

The name of the town of Cahir is a short version of the Irish for 'Fortress of the Dun Abounding in Fish', and its setting, on the River Suir, is both attractive and strategic. The seemingly impregnable **Cahir Castle** (charge; www.heritageireland.ie) guards the crucial crossing. Built on the river's lovely islet – a site fortified since the third century – the present castle dates from the fifteenth century. It's in a fine state of restoration, and guided tours point out military details, such as musket slits, a portcullis and a cannonball embedded high in one of the walls. While you're in Cahir, take a look at **Swiss Cottage** (charge; www.heritageireland.ie), an early nineteenth-century romantic cottage, in the bright Regency style. It has been fully restored right down to the thatched roof and original French wallpaper.

CASHEL

In **Cashel ⓮**, Co Tipperary, monastic ruins crown an imposing hilltop. The **Rock of Cashel** (charge; www.heritageireland.ie) is a 61m- (200ft-) high outcrop of limestone, where the kings of Munster had their headquarters from the fourth to the twelfth centuries; it's also where St Patrick visited in 450 and baptised King Aengus and his brothers. In 1101 ecclesiastical authorities built an Irish-Romanesque church here, **Cormac's Chapel** (consecrated in 1134), which is unique in that it was built by Irish monks who interpreted architectural styles they had studied in Europe. It features a steeply pitched stone roof, rows of blank arches and two oddly positioned towers, while stone-carvings of beasts and abstract designs decorate the doorway and arches.

The chapel is dwarfed by the **cathedral** that abuts it. This structure, dating from the thirteenth century, has thick and well-preserved walls, but the roof collapsed during the eighteenth century. On the positive side, the resulting hole lets the sunlight stream in, helping to clarify the many architectural details, as well as the exquisite medieval stone-carvings.

Inside the entrance, St Patrick's Cross is one of the oldest crosses in Ireland, and it looks like it – the sculptures on both sides are very weather-beaten. The cross rises up from the 'Coronation Stone', said to have been a pagan sacrificial altar.

It was in the lively market town of Thurles, in 1174, that the Irish forces defeated the Anglo-Norman army led by Strongbow (see page 22). Seven hundred years later, the town saw the birth of the Gaelic Athletic Association (GAA), now an amateur sports organisation with 500,000 members worldwide. If you wish to learn more about the games history, pay a visit to the Lár na Páirce GAA Museum (charge; http://larnapairce.ie). **Thurles'** most conspicuous landmark is the Catholic Cathedral, which was built in a nineteenth-century version of the Romanesque style; its square bell tower, 38m (125ft) high, can be seen for miles around.

On the west bank of the River Suir, 6km (4 miles) south of Thurles is the Cistercian **Holy Cross Abbey**. Construction of the church here, which is still in use, started in Romanesque style, but slowly evolved into Gothic. The solid white walls, enhanced by window-tracery, reach up to a perfectly restored fifteenth-century ceiling, while a triple-arched recess contains seats of honour carved from jet-black marble and is decorated with ancient coats of arms. Another detail is the night stairs, down which the monks stumbled from their sleeping quarters at 2am to chant matins. One of the bells in the tower was cast in the early thirteenth century, making it Ireland's oldest.

Kilkenny Castle

KILKENNY

Unquestionably Ireland's most atmospheric medieval city, **Kilkenny** ⓯ straddles the broad River Nore, doglegging past its striking castle. This was the capital of the old Kingdom of Ossory, a relatively small realm in pre-Norman Ireland.

Parliament, which convened here in 1366, passed the notorious but ineffectual Statutes of Kilkenny, with the aim of segregating the Irish from the Anglo-Normans (in those days intermarriage was seen as high treason). In the seventeenth century an independent Irish parliament met here for several years, and in 1650, Oliver

Cromwell took the town for the English, suffering heavy losses in the process.

The Irish *Cill Choinnigh* means St Canice's church; **St Canice's Cathedral**, built in the thirteenth century, is on the original site of the church, which gave the town its name. Though Cromwell's rampaging troops badly damaged the building, it has since been restored to an admirable state. In the churchyard stands a graceful ninth-century Round Tower, the only vestige of St Canice's monastic settlement

Kilkenny Castle (www.kilkennycastle.ie) was built in the thirteenth century to replace the primitive fortress erected by Strongbow, before it was taken over by the Butler family, one of the great Anglo-Norman dynasties. Inside, you'll be able to see the impressive hall, whose chequered floor is tiled with black Kilkenny marble, as well as a library, drawing room and nineteenth-century-style bedrooms. The ornate Georgian stable of the Castle Yard houses the headquarters of the Design and Crafts Council Ireland (www.dcci.ie), which mounts a varied programme of exhibitions by Irish and international craftspeople, ranging from stained glass to quilts.

Heading down the Parade from the castle and across the junction to the High Street leads past the Tholsel (city hall), and, subsequently, town hall, constructed in 1761. The High Street blends seamlessly into Parliament Street, both replete with shops and cafés. The finest remnant of the city's Tudor prosperity is **Rothe House and Garden** (charge; http://rothehouse.com), a complex of three dwellings linked by courtyards. Behind the house, two walled gardens – one for vegetables and herbs, the other a still immature orchard – have been restored to their early seventeenth-century state.

Just outside of **Thomastown** you can visit the partially restored ruins of the Cistercian **Jerpoint Abbey** (charge; www.heritage ireland.ie). Founded in the mid-twelfth century by the King of

St Finbarr's Cathedral in Cork City

Ossory, it had a brief, troubled history before succumbing to the dissolution of the monasteries in 1540. Parts of it retain their Romanesque lines, but the square central tower with its stepped battlements was added during the fifteenth century. Much of the sculptural work in the cloister and church is intact, and you can see larger-than-life carvings of knights and saints, which are inspiring monuments both to those they honour, and to the talented and devoted sculptors who worked here in the Middle Ages.

From Thomastown, make the journey to the picturesque village of **Inistioge**, just 7km (5 miles) away and the location for famous films such as *The Secret Scripture* starring Rooney Mara, Vanessa Redgrave, Aidan Turner, and Eric Bana, and *Widow's Peak* with Mia Farrow. While you're here, **Woodstock Gardens & Arboretum** are perfect for a scenic woodland walk.

Cobh harbour

THE SOUTHWEST

HIGHLIGHTS

- Cork, see page 64
- County Cork, see page 65
- County Kerry, see page 70
- Ring of Kerry, see page 71

CORK

Ireland's largest county marries gently rolling farmland with rugged, stony peninsulas and delightful bays. Enclosed by steep hills, **Cork City** ⓰ has all the facilities of an important commercial and industrial centre, but its atmosphere is unique. The River Lee divides into two channels to the west of the city centre, leaving the centre on an island connected to its north and south banks by numerous bridges, with seagulls flying overhead and swans gliding by.

The city's name is an anglicisation of *Corcaigh* 'Marshy Place' which is how the area looked in the sixth century when St Finbarr arrived to found a church and school. In the year 820 the Vikings raided marshy Cork, destroying the institutions and houses, and because they liked the lay of the land, they returned to build their own town on the same site. This destruction and rebuilding repeated like a pattern in the seventeenth century and then again during the Irish War of Independence 1919–21.

Cork's beauty begs slow exploration and one can easily spend the day strolling along its narrow canals and winding streets. Patrick Street, fondly known as 'Pana' by locals is the wide main street of Cork. Curved because it was built above a river channel, it makes for great window-shopping anytime and is full of people promenading on Saturday afternoons. A venture across the south channel of the River Lee will take you to St Finbarr's Cathedral, the latest version of which was built in the nineteenth century and follows the lofty French-Gothic style, with arches upon arches. Across the river's north channel on the Christy Ring Bridge and up the hill is St Anne's Church, home to the Shandon Bells and clock tower, fondly known to locals as the 'four-faced liar' due to the apparent disparity in the time being shown on its different sides. Visitors can climb up through the clockwork intricacies and even play a tune on the bells.

Nearby, at Sunday's Well, you can visit the fully restored nineteenth- and early twentieth-century cells of the Cork

NOTES

Kinsale was under siege in 1601 as Spanish troops, who had sailed to aid the Irish against Queen Elizabeth, were defeated, ultimately sparking the 'flight of the Earls' (the exodus of the Irish nobility) in 1607, and the redistribution of their lands.

City Gaol (charge; http://corkcitygaol.com), which operated until 1923 when Republican prisoners were released after the Civil War. The same building high above the city was the location of Cork's first radio station, and now hosts a delightfully idiosyncratic radio museum.

COUNTY CORK

Cork is a good centre for excursions, not least **Blarney Castle** ⓱ (charge; www.blarneycastle.ie) 8km (5 miles) to the west. Allegedly capable of bestowing the 'gift of the gab' (eloquence), the famous Blarney Stone is kissed by many tourists every day. One of many competing origin stories claims that this is part of the Stone of Scone, gifted to the chieftain Cormac MacCarthy by Robert the Bruce in gratitude for his assistance in the 1314 battle of Bannockburn. To kiss the awkwardly placed stone you need to climb up to the battlement, lie flat on your back, hang on to two iron bars and extend your head backwards.

The castle itself is worth a visit, even if hordes of tourists do besiege it every summer. The formidable keep was built in the middle of the fifteenth century, while the private park, in which the castle stands, includes a grove of ancient yew trees, said to be a site of Druid worship.

Cobh ⓲, the seaport of Cork city, lies about 24km (15 miles) east of Cork City; it is pronounced 'Cove', which is exactly what it means in Irish. From Queen Victoria's 1849 visit until 1922, Cobh was called Queenstown.

The port is touched by nostalgia – from the tragic traffic of desperate emigrants fleeing the Great Famine for Canada or America to the days of the great transatlantic liners (this was the last port of departure for the ill-fated *Titanic*). **The Queenstown Story** (charge www.cobhheritage.com) relays Cobh's long and often tragic seafaring history, while the **Titanic Experience** (charge; www.titanic experiencecobh.ie) has some interesting audiovisuals, including

The Old Head of Kinsale

footage of the wreck, discovered in 1985, passenger stories and eyewitness accounts. High above the harbour, the spire of the **Cathedral of St Colman** reaches heavenward. Recitals are given in the summer on the cathedral's 47-bell carillon.

In Midleton, to the northeast of Cobh, the Midleton Distillery Experience (charge; www.jamesonwhiskey.com) offers tours and tastings in a converted whiskey distillery that dates back to the late eighteenth century, and which has been occupied by Jameson since 1975.

The town of Youghal (in English pronounced 'Yawl'), east of Midleton, also has a long seafaring history, but today is best known for its 8km (5mile) -long sandy beach. On the site of the main town gate is the attractive **clock tower**, dating from 1776 and formerly a prison where rebels were hanged from the windows to set an

The Ring of Kerry

example to the populace. The high street runs right through it with the structure's four narrow floors and belfry rising above an arched platform over the street.

The most impressive monument in Youghal, **St Mary's Collegiate Church** (Church of Ireland) stands on the site of the fifth-century monastic settlement of St Declan of Ardmore, and is one of the oldest functioning churches in Ireland, built in about 1250. Among the monuments and tombs in the church is one built, in his own honour, by Richard Boyle, an Elizabethan adventurer and the first Earl of Cork. On Market Square, the tourist office is attached to the heritage centre (www.youghal.ie), which recounts the port's history since the ninth century.

Enjoying a glorious setting at the head of a sheltered harbour around the mouth of the Bandon River, **Kinsale** ⓳, about 29km

(18 miles) south of Cork, is a joy to sailors and sightseers alike. It's also renowned for its restaurants, which are among the best in southwest Ireland.

Kinsale's most compelling sight is the formidable star-shaped **Charles Fort** (charge; www.heritageireland.ie), whose eerie roofless shells are substantial enough to give a ready impression of what life in the fort must have been like for its garrison of four hundred. The **town museum** (free) is immediately recognizable in the warren of lanes at the centre of town by its Dutch-style triple gables.

Migratory birds flock to the **Old Head** of Kinsale, 16km (10 miles) beyond the town where a modern lighthouse stands as the successor to a beacon dating back to pre-Christian times. It was off the Old Head that a German submarine torpedoed the world-famous liner, the *Lusitania*, on 7 May 1915, resulting in the loss of 1,500 lives.

Clonakilty, another coastal town situated between Kinsale and Bantry, is home to the West Cork Model Railway Village (charge; www.modelvillage.ie), which replicates the 1940s, but now defunct, West Cork Railway and the towns it served in great detail at 1:24 scale.

Nestling between steep green hills and a tranquil bay, the town of Bantry's main sight is **Bantry House and Garden** (charge; www.bantryhouse.com), a part-Georgian, part-Victorian stately home full of tapestries, paintings and furnishings and set in sub-tropical gardens.

Heading counter-clockwise around the bay from Bantry, the highway weaves through more rocky hills until it descends upon **Glengarriff ⑳**, where the beauty of the setting and the pleasant climate account for its year-round popularity.

Boat trips (www.bluepoolferry.ie; www.harbourqueenferry.com) touted by traditional boatmen in Glengarriff cruise past Seal Island, and you can opt to land on Garnish Island (Apr–Oct daily times vary; www.garnishisland.com) a 15-hectare (37-acre) garden. The flora comes from five continents, and the centrepiece is a walled

Italian garden, surrounding a pool, with the gentle air of a paradisiacal perfume factory. Until 1910, Garnish was a bleak military outpost, and from the top of the Martello tower, sentries once kept a lookout for Napoleonic invasion fleets; today, you can survey the luxuriant hills around the bay.

COUNTY KERRY

By any standard this is a spectacular part of the world: the Atlantic in all its moods, lakes designed for lovers or poets, and steep, evergreen mountains. **Killarney** ㉑ is a good base from which to explore the area, and seeing the sights here can be accomplished in many ways – by car, coach, bicycle, boat or even by 'jaunting car' – a horse-drawn rig driven by a *jarvey* (guide) who knows the territory and how to tell a story.

It is best to visit the **Gap of Dunloe**, a wild gorge 6km (4 miles) long, on a fully organised excursion, usually a half-day trip; the Gap can be traversed on a pony, in a pony trap or on foot. Sound effects underline the weirdness of the eerie rock-strewn scenery as echoes bounce off the mountains – **MacGillycuddy's Reeks** in the west (the highest range in Ireland), and to the east, **Purple Mountain**. The long trek leads to the shore of the Upper Lake, where the tour continues by boat to Ross Castle. The scenery around the lakes – thick forests, stark crags and enchanted islands – could not be more romantic, but there's adventure, too: the **rapids** at Old Weir Bridge.

Muckross Abbey is a friary dating from the fifteenth century with a massive square tower, a cloister with Gothic arches on two sides, Norman or Romanesque on the others and an old, weathered yew tree. From the friary, continue to Muckross House (charge; www.muckross-house.ie), where guided tours lead visitors around the rich Victorian interiors of this fine nineteenth-century neo-Elizabethan stately home. On the other side of the car park are the three traditional **working farms** where you can chat to actors playing out the roles of farmers and their wives.

RING OF KERRY

The **Ring of Kerry** ㉒ may well be the most sensational 180km (112 miles) you have ever driven. A circular route around a coast of rugged cliffs and enthralling seascapes, this round-trip can be made in either direction, but here we proceed clockwise. Set aside a whole day to really make the most of it.

Leaving Killarney, the road goes past lush lakeland. **Kenmare** is famous for lacemaking and the fish that fill the estuary. North of the small resort of Castlecove, 3km (2 miles) off the main road, are the ruins of **Staigue Fort**; a 2,500-year-old stronghold and one of Ireland's main archaeological wonders, this almost circular structure measures about 27m (90ft) across with a 6m- (18ft-) high wall.

Near Caherdaniel, **Derrynane House**, the home of popular, non-violent campaigner Daniel O'Connell (see page 25), has been fully restored and is now a museum (charge; www.derrynanehouse.ie). The plain, elegant house, which was largely rebuilt by the "Liberator" himself when he inherited it in 1825, contains all manner of memorabilia, as well as a tea room and a lively, 25-minute audiovisual that's well worth catching.

From the mainland at Portmagee, a bridge connects to **Valentia Island**, which was the European terminus of the first transatlantic cable (1866), making

Slea Head on the Dingle Peninsula

NOTES

To the east of Tralee, the town of Castleisland is the location of the Crag Cave (charge; www.cragcave.com). Nearly 4km (2.5 miles) long and bristling with stalagmites and stalactites, this is one of the best show caves in Ireland.

possible telegraphic contact with America. At the western edge of the village, the **Valentia Island Heritage Centre** (charge; http://vhc.cablehistory.org) houses a display on the island's history in the old primary school.

Off Valentia, the **Skelligs Islands** rise abruptly from the ocean, shrouded with mystery and birds; a voyage here is one of the most exciting and inspiring trips you can make in Ireland. Skellig Michael and its monastic ruins, a UNESCO World Heritage Site, provided the setting for scenes in two Star Wars films (*The Force Awakens* and *The Last Jedi*). Operators to the island include Skellig Michael Cruises (http://skelligmichaelcruises.com) and John O'Shea (http://skelligtours.com).

On the north shore of the peninsula, hills plunge to sea level and cliffs complete the descent. **Dingle Bay** seems startlingly wide and the Dingle Peninsula looks like another country. From Glenbeigh to Killorglin, the head of the bay is almost totally protected from the rough sea by huge sandbars extending from either shore. **Rossbeigh Strand**, with its 6km (4 miles) of golden sand, is a dream beach.

The last town on the ring, **Killorglin**, saves all its energy for three days in August and a boisterous pagan pageant called the Puck Fair (http://puckfair.ie), during which time a mountain goat presides over round-the-clock festivities. To the north, **Tralee** ㉓, the administrative centre of County Kerry, owes its fame to the songwriter William Mulchinock (1820–64) whose *The Rose of Tralee* inspired the eponymous annual festival (www.roseoftralee.ie) in late August.

Kerry County Museum (charge; www.kerrymuseum.ie) in Tralee incorporates a comprehensive run-through of the history of Ireland and Kerry since the Stone Age, as well as the Medieval Experience, a series of re-created scenes of mid-fifteenth-century Tralee complete with artificial smells.

Tralee is the principal gateway to the Dingle Peninsula, a long, dramatic finger pointing some 48km (30 miles) into the Atlantic Ocean. On the south shore, amidst rocky coves, a sandbar grows into an arc of beach jutting more than halfway across the bay. Inch Strand's 6km (4 miles) of sand slide gently into the sea. Behind the bathers, archaeologists putter about the dunes, where inhabitants of prehistoric ages left meaningful clues about their way of life.

The small fishing port and resort of **Dingle** ㉔ (officially known

King John's Castle in Limerick

as *An Daingean*, the name to look for on signposts) claims to be the most westerly town in Europe. From here to land's end all the hamlets are Irish-speaking parts of the *Gaeltacht* (see page 132), where folklore and traditional language are still preserved. This is rugged farming country, where old stone walls are overgrown with shrubs, thick hedges divide skimpy parcels of land into fields and hardy sheep graze on even the most precipitous of hills.

The western part of the peninsula is rich territory for archaeologists. In one area, the Fahan group alone consists of an astonishing four hundred *clocháns* (beehive-shaped stone huts), along with forts and other ancient structures. For a spectacular panorama, drive up the **Conor Pass** (at an altitude of 460m/1,500ft) and see the sea out to the north and south, and mountains and lakes on

The extraordinary landscape of the Burren

the east and west sides. In this part of the world you're isolated from everything but the wild fuchsia and heather beside the road.

THE WEST

HIGHLIGHTS

» Limerick and Clare, see page 75
» The Burren, see page 77
» Galway, see page 79
» Connemara, see page 81
» Aran Islands, see page 83
» County Mayo, see page 85

LIMERICK AND CLARE

By the time the waters of the River Shannon have reached **Limerick** ㉕ in the west, they have flowed over 274km (170 miles) across all terrains, from narrow streams and swirling rapids to lakes and lochs. After Limerick they still have another 97km (60 miles) to travel through the estuary to the open Atlantic.

Limerick's position at the meeting of the river and its tidal waters assured the city experienced a long and often violent history. The Danes were first on the scene, although their belligerence provoked repeated attacks by the native Irish, who finally drove them out. The Anglo-Normans in turn captured *Luimneach* – in English 'Bare Spot' – and in 1210 King John visited and ordered the construction of a bridge and King John's Castle (charge; www.kingjohnscastle.ie), which still survive and have been extensively renovated; a shiny **visitor centre** has facilitated the castle's twenty-first-century rebirth, bringing fresh life into the building with dazzling new displays. The city endured its most memorable siege after the **Battle of the Boyne** (1690), when Irish supporters of James II (see page 97) retreated to Limerick, pursued by

A gargoyle on Lynch's Castle in Galway

William of Orange. They lost, but the Treaty of Limerick allowed them to leave with honour and guaranteed the Irish freedom of religion This was repudiated by the English Parliament, so today Limerick carries the title of 'City of the Violated Treaty'.

The 850-year-old St Mary's Cathedral (free; www.saintmaryscathedral.ie) has an arched Irish-Romanesque west door, while fifteenth-century carved misericords under the choir seats show free-ranging imagination, with representations of angels, animals, and other figures in relief. The waterfront Custom House is now the Hunt Museum (charge; www.huntmuseum.com), housing an outstanding collection of Celtic and medieval treasures and a selection of twentieth-century Irish and European art, including works by Picasso and Renoir.

By the entrance to the People's Park stands the **Limerick City Gallery of Art** (free; www.gallery.limerick.ie), which has been remodelled with renovated galleries. Displayed on a rotating basis, the permanent collection of eighteenth- to twenty-first-century paintings and drawings by artists such as Sean Keating, Paul Henry and Jack Butler Yeats will appeal to aficionados of Irish art.

West of Limerick, bypassed by the main N18 Ennis road, lies the village of **Bunratty,** where **Bunratty Castle and Folk Park** ㉖ (charge; www. bunrattycastle.ie) form one of Ireland's most popular attractions. In the evenings, **"medieval banquets"** are staged here, as the lords and ladies of the castle welcome guests for an evening of music, mead and merriment. The expansive castle grounds host the **folk park**, a re-creation of a nineteenth-century village, replete with post office, shops, a church and a pub, all populated by actors in period dress.

Ennis, the county town of county Clare, has a thirteenth-century friary, which in the Middle Ages had 350 friars and 600 students. Better still, the town has decent restaurants, a joyous range of bookshops and independent boutiques and, above all, a thriving **traditional music** session scene – indeed it stages two major festivals: the **Fleadh Nua** (www.fleadhnua.com), over the last week of May, and the **Ennis Traditional Music Festival** (www.ennistradfest.com), which runs for five days in early November

THE BURREN

Northwest of Ennis, around 520sq km (200sq miles) of County Clare belongs to **the Burren** ㉗, where glaciers and ages of erosion have created limestone pavements – horizontal slabs divided by fissures, like the aftermath of an earthquake. Though sometimes described as a moonscape, the Burren is anything but barren; it is a quiet world of small animals, birds, butterflies, and alpine and Mediterranean flowers. It may seem hostile to human habitation, but the profusion of forts and tombs proves it supported a population for several centuries.

Geologists, botanists and archaeologists have field trips on the pavements, and speleologists enjoy the caves, of which more than 40km (25 miles) have been

NOTES

A frustrated general serving under Oliver Cromwell famously condemned the desolate Burren as having 'not enough wood to hang a man, not enough water to drown him, not enough clay to cover his corpse'.

NOTES

The surnames of the 14 families or 'tribes' of Welsh and Norman descent who controlled medieval Galway are still commonly found in the city: Blake, Bodkin, Browne, D'Arcy, Ffrench, Kirwan, Joyce, Lynch, Morris, Martin, Skerrett, Athy, Dean and Ffont.

fully explored. Most are for experts only, but anyone can visit Aillwee Cave, south-east of Ballyvaughan (www.aillweeburrenexperience.ie). The **Burren Centre** (www.theburrencentre.ie) provides an entertaining account of the area's history, with its "In a Walk through Time" exhibition. There's also an exhibition on traditional music from Kilfenora, focusing on the **Kilfenora** Ceili Band, Ireland's oldest and most illustrious ceili band.

Towering 215m (700ft) over the Atlantic Ocean, the **Cliffs of Moher** ㉘, 10km (6 miles) extend some 8km from Hag's Head, west of Liscannor, to a little beyond **O'Brien's Tower**, which was constructed in 1835 at their highest point. Hidden within the hillside, the visitor centre (charge; www.cliffsofmoher.ie) houses the Atlantic Edge exhibition whose interactive touch screens, computer games and 3-D film do in part provide lucid explanations of the cliffs' evolution and wildlife. In the opposite direction to O'Brien's Tower, a **viewing platform** offers the best sight of the wave-battered cliffs below, enhanced by the resonant roar of the Atlantic waves pummelling the rocks at shore level

The town of Lisdoonvarna was once famous as a spa, but today is chiefly known for its Matchmaking Festival (www.matchmakerireland.com) in September after the harvest, when farmers traditionally took a break from farming to seek a wife. The festival is a light-hearted affair, attracting some 40,000 hopeful visitors annually.

Across the border in County Galway, the area around Gort has a number of literary associations. Lady Gregory, co-founder of the Abbey Theatre, lived in **Coole Park** (charge; www.coolepark.

ie) where a unique 'autograph tree' is inscribed with the initials of some of her famous visitors – Augustus John, John Masefield, Sean O'Casey and one of the few who is instantly recognized by his initials: George Bernard Shaw.

GALWAY

The main city of the western province of Connaught, **Galway** ㉙ is a port, resort, administrative and cultural centre. In medieval times it prospered as a city-state, but withered in the seventeenth century after prolonged sieges by the forces of Oliver Cromwell and, four decades later, by William of Orange. Remnants of the old glory still shine in a few corners of the renewed city, with its vibrant young population.

The Collegiate **Church of St Nicholas** (charge; http://stnicholas.ie) was begun by the Anglo-Normans in 1320 and is dedicated to the patron saint of seafarers, Saint Nicholas of Myra. According to local legend, Columbus came to pray here in 1477, long before his voyage to America. Today the area around the church hosts a lively weekend food and craft market (http://galwaymarket.com).

During Galway's heyday, fourteen families – mostly of Welsh and Norman descent – formed a sort of medieval Mafia that controlled the

Derryclare Lake in Connemara

Inishmore from above

economic and political life of the town. Their common enemy, the O'Flaherty family, inspired the inscription (1549) over the old town gate: 'From the fury of the O'Flaherties, good Lord deliver us'. Of the tribes in Galway, the Lynch family left the most memories and monuments, including Lynch's Castle, a town house dating from 1600 decorated with excellent stonework, gargoyles and carved window frames. This superb building has been restored and now houses a bank.

Another reminder of the Lynches is the **Lynch Memorial Window** in Market St, with a plaque recounting the macabre story of James Lynch Fitzstephen – Mayor of Galway in 1493 – who condemned and executed his own son, Walter, for murder. Judge Lynch had to be the hangman because nobody else would agree to carry out the sentence.

Galway's Catholic cathedral – whose full name is the **Cathedral of Our Lady Assumed into Heaven and St Nicholas** – (donation requested; www.galwaycathedral.ie) has a giant dome looming over the city – the classical architecture is misleading; the church was dedicated in 1965. Alongside the cathedral is Galway's Salmon Weir, in which salmon fight their way from the sea up to Lough Corrib. From June to July you can see them queueing up for a chance to leap up the falls and follow their instincts to sweet water.

About 1km southwest of Wolfe Tone Bridge begins the resort suburb of **Salthill**, Galway's summer playground, home to a long promenade and a clean sandy beach. It's a great place to watch the sun set on Galway Bay; sprawling hills enclose most of the bay, but the Atlantic can be seen to the west.

CONNEMARA

Lough Corrib, which extends 43km (27 miles) north from Galway, is big enough to be whipped by waves when the wind hurtles down the hillside. It's generally shallow and well supplied with islands and fish – salmon, trout, pike and perch. **Lough Corrib** divides County Galway into two contrasting regions: a fertile limestone plain to the east, and Connemara – a range of dramatic mountains and sparkling lakes – to the west, all enclosed by the coastline of rugged cliffs and pristine beaches.

Much of the south coast of Connemara is an Irish-speaking enclave, as well as being the home of the Connemara pony – robust, intelligent and self-reliant. Spanish horses of the sixteenth century are rumoured to have crossbred with Irish ponies; one version says that

NOTES

The huge Twelve Bens of Connemara ('ben' is Gaelic for peak) constitute a range of moody mountains mostly inhabited by sheep; the foothills are interspersed with bogs and pretty lakes.

Croagh Patrick

the stallions swam ashore from ships when the Spanish Armada wrecked on nearby rocks.

The sky seems to change by the minute in the far west – dazzling sun, fleeting clouds and rain alternating so quickly that photographers have to be constantly at the ready. The capital is the well-placed market town of **Clifden** ㉚, a base for exploring the nearby lakes and rivers, as well as fine beaches, bogs and mountains; the town's Irish name is *An Clochán*, meaning 'Stepping Stones'. There are so many areas of water around Clifden that you can't tell the genuine sea inlets from the coves of the lakes, except for the seaweed, a plant that features in Irish cooking more than you'd expect (usually called '*dulse*' or '*dillisk*'). Nearby is Kylemore Abbey (visitor centre free, gardens and abbey charge; www.kylemoreabbey.com), the home of Ireland's Benedictine nuns.

ARAN ISLANDS

Out in the Atlantic, 48km (30 miles) off Galway, the **Aran Islands** ㉛ (www.aranislands.ie) are a remote outpost indeed, little more than stone outcrops. In the past islanders had to struggle to survive, cultivating the bleak limestone terrain, which had so little topsoil that they would ship it in from the mainland or scrape it from the

CRUISING THE RIVER SHANNON

The best place to hire a boat is Carrick-on-Shannon, the capital of County Leitrim and home to the superb Costello Memorial Chape, supposedly the smallest chapel in Europe. Downstream, the river runs into Lough Corry, the first of many interconnected lakes in the Shannon basin. Lough Ree, halfway down, is 26km- (16 miles-) long and 11km- (7 miles-) wide, with deserted wooded islands.

The main cross-country roads ford the Shannon at the central market town of Athlone, with a medieval castle overlooking the Shannon Bridge. At a bend in the river is Clonmacnoise, an ancient monastic settlement founded in the sixth century by St Ciaran.

Just 6km (4 miles) south of Clonmacnoise, a 16-arch bridge marks Shannonbridge; at Shannon Harbour the Grand Canal from Dublin meets the river. Portumna is an easy-going boating resort, with a fine castle and forest park.

Lough Derg is the largest of the Shannon lakes – 40km- (25 miles-) long and up to 5km- (3 miles-) wide with islets and fair green hills beyond – a perfect end to the trip. This is just as well because dangerous rapids abound below Killaloe, a prudent place to abandon ship. Killaloe was once a great ecclesiastical centre, where St Flannan's Cathedral has been restored to its twelfth-century glory. The richly carved Romanesque doorway is said to be the entrance to the tomb of King Murtagh O'Brien of Munster (d. 1120). The granite shaft nearby, from circa 1000, bears a bilingual inscription in Runic and Ogham letters – a foretaste of today's Irish-English road signs.

cracks between the rocks and mix it with seaweed fertiliser to grow feed for their livestock. Tourism has now improved their fortunes, and though their famous Aran sweaters are still made here, these days few of them are hand-knitted. All the locals speak Gaelic in their daily life, but can also speak English.

Inishmore, 'the Big Island', is 14km- (9 miles-) from tip to tip and only 3km- (2 miles-) across. From the air – and you can fly there from Galway (www.aerarannislands.ie) – you can make out tapestries of tiny fields enclosed by dry-stone walls. The fishermen work aboard modern trawlers, but the traditional *currachs*, tar-coated boats with canvas hulls, are still used. Ferries dock at **Kilronan**, the main village, from where you can rent a bicycle – the best way to explore the island. But if you're in a hurry, you can hire pony traps

Aerial view of Dún Aengus, Aran Islands

for guided tours, or there's a minibus that does journeys all around the island.

The island's most remarkable monument is **Dún Aengus** (charge; http://heritageireland.ie), a semicircular fort of three concentric enclosures, hard up against the edge of sheer, 90m-high cliffs. The **inner citadel** comprises a wall, 6m high and 4m wide, of massive blocks of limestone that were quarried on site and put together without mortar. Even in modern times it would take a rash general to stage an attack on Dún Aengus.

Elsewhere on the islands, among colourful wild flowers, grazing cows, sheep and an abundance of bounding rabbits, there are numerous archaeological sites of minor importance that nevertheless have their own diversion to offer. Here you'll find stone forts and groups of primitive stone dwellings, as well as hermits' cells, round towers, holy wells, and ruined churches.

Inis Oírr (http://discoverinisoirr.com) is the smallest island with a beautiful, sandy beach, while the **lighthouse** at the southeastern tip of the island affords fantastic views of the Cliffs of Moher. Inis Oírr will be instantly recognisable to fans of the TV classic 'Father Ted' as Craggy Island, look out for the Tedfest celebrations (http://tedfest.org) every March. Otherwise, an innovative arts centre, **Aras Eanna** (www.aras-eanna.ie/en), shows temporary art exhibitions and runs demonstrations of traditional basket-making and weaving, as well as hosting some of Ireland's top acts.

COUNTY MAYO

Rising high above Clew Bay, conical Croagh Patrick is Ireland's holy mountain, and where St Patrick is said to have spent Lent here in 441. Major **pilgrimages** take place three times a year: on March 17 (St Patrick's Day), August 15 (Assumption Day) and – the main event – on the last Sunday in July, when tens of thousands of pilgrims make the climb to attend Mass on the summit, some fasting and barefoot. On a fine day the mountain offers an awesome

SHAMROCK CURTAIN

Travelling in the west of Ireland you may cross the Shamrock Curtain, an important cultural frontier. Signs are printed in Gaelic letters and the people speak Irish as a first language; this is the Gaeltacht. Its residents strive to maintain Irish as a living language, while the Dublin government actively supports Gaeltacht efforts to keep the old language and culture alive. Courses in Irish offered here every summer are a rite of passage for Irish teenagers.

panorama, stretching from the Twelve Bens in the south to Slieve League in the north.

Westport ㉜, at the head of Clew Bay, is a fine example of eighteenth-century urban planning. It was laid out in classical style in 1780 for the Browne family of Westport House by James Wyatt, who built a striking octagonal square and canalized the Carrowbeg River, flanking it with the tree-lined Mall. The town's focal point is **Westport House** (charge; www.westporthouse.ie), a graceful Georgian mansion now surrounded by a country park of rides and amusements; on the estate is a host of **attractions,** such as a miniature railway, a log flume ride and swan pedaloes

To the east of Castlebar, a quiet partly Georgian town, is **The National Museum of Ireland – Country Life** ㉝ (free; www.museum.ie) houses the National Folklife Collection, a series of hugely entertaining displays illustrating rural life in Ireland from 1850 to about 1950.

Inland, the village of **Knock** (from the Irish *Cnoc Mhuire* – 'Mary's Hill') is a another venerated place of pilgrimage. In 1879 the townspeople saw an apparition of the Virgin Mary, St Joseph and St John on a south gable of the old parish church, and in the centenary year of 1979, pilgrim Pope John Paul II came from Rome to address an open-air mass at Knock with over 400,000 of the faithful. Knock still caters to the pilgrims, with souvenir shops and a museum of folklore and handicrafts. The site of the famous apparition has been enclosed in glass, and statues recreate the position of the figures in the vision.

In Foxford, the old woollen mill houses an interpretative centre that tells the story of the famine in the area, while near Ballycastle, on the north Mayo cliffs, the pyramid-shaped heritage centre of **Céide Fields** (charge; www.ceidefields.com) uncovers the site of one of the area's many prehistoric settlements. The site, dating back to 3000 BC, is estimated to be the single largest Stone Age monument in existence in the world today.

The country's biggest island, **Achill** ㉞, is buffeted by wind and tide, with meagre farms between ominous mountains and rocky shores. Despite this (or because of it) the scenery – from enormous cliffs to superb beaches – is truly magnificent. Achill feels adrift, though you can drive there from the mainland across an unimpressive bridge. Driving on the island's deserted roads can revive the joy of motoring.

Prehistoric graves can be found on the harsh slopes of Achill's overpoweringly high mountain, the 672-m (2,204-ft) Slievemore. Driving offers the most vertigo-inducing cliff views and perspectives of the ocean churning round the off-islands and shoals. Inland, note the three-chimneyed cottages set between moors and bogs.

Sligo town

THE NORTHWEST

HIGHLIGHTS

» County Donegal, see page 89

Lying between two mountains, Ben Bulben and Knocknarea, **Sligo** ㉟ rose to prominence following the Anglo-Norman invasion of Connacht in 1235. In 1252, Maurice Fitzgerald, the Earl of Kildare, founded **Sligo Abbey** (charge; www.heritageireland.ie), a Dominican friary that was burned down in 1414. Rebuilt soon after, it was attacked by Puritan troops in 1641 and the friars killed. With three sides remaining, a delicately decorated **high altar** and some fine carvings, its present ruins combine desolation and grace.

Eight kilometres west of Sligo town and set against the backdrop of Knocknarea Mountain, seaside **Strandhill** boasts a gorgeous situation, its beach boasting long-rolling waves for surfers. At 328-m (1,078-ft) high, **Knocknarea** is a steep but manageable climb, and at the summit is a large cairn believed to mark the burial place of the first-century Queen Maeve of Connaught. This vantage point gives a fantastic, sweeping view across Sligo Bay. Awesome **Ben Bulben** looms in the distance, 526m- (1,730ft-) high, its flat top covered in arctic and alpine plants.

In the shadow of this majestic mountain is the small church of Drumcliff, with its turreted belfry. It was the desire of **W.B. Yeats**, who spent many childhood summer holidays around Sligo, to be laid to rest in the churchyard, 'Under bare Ben Bulben's head'.

About 27km (17 miles) to the north of Sligo, situated on the approach to the village of Mullaghmore, look out for the stunning **Classiebawn Castle**, which claims the skyline all to itself. This was the summer dwelling of Earl Mountbatten of Burma, who was assassinated by the IRA in 1979 when his fishing boat was blown up just off the shore nearby.

COUNTY DONEGAL

The most northerly county on the island, **Donegal** is known for its scenery – mountains, glens and lakes. **Donegal town** ❸❻ has a medieval castle that occupies the site of a previous Viking fort; *Dun na nGall* in Irish means the 'Fortress of the Foreigners', a reference to the Vikings. On the edge of town, the ruins of Donegal Abbey overlook the estuary. West along the coast, **Killybegs** was once the most successful fishing port in Ireland, but these it's known more as a destination for major cruise liners.

The road to the village of **Glencolumbkille** ❸❼ heads deep into spectacular country. Over the crest of a hill, you see the simple village below, enfolded in green hillsides that funnel down to the sea – in Irish, the name *Glencolumbkille* means the 'Glen of St Colmcille'

Charming Donegal town

(or St Columba).

Today it is said that the sixth-century saint, who changed the course of history by introducing the Christian faith to Scotland, began his career by converting locals. The numerous old standing stones were formerly pagan monuments, which St Columba simply adapted to the new religion. On the saint's feast day, 9 June, pilgrims follow the pathway of these old stones. Over forty prehistoric *dolmens, souterrains* and cairns have been catalogued in this area, some as old as 5,000 years.

Perched on a hilltop in Inishowen, you can visit the **Grianan Aileach Ring Fort** dating from 1700 BC; well-preserved, it's similar in style to Staigue Fort in Co Kerry. Fort Dunree, on the Inishowen peninsula overlooking Lough Swilly, is a fascinating military history museum in an old fort.

Glenveagh National Park 38 (www.nationalparks.ie/glenveagh) sprawls across 10,000 hectares (24,700 acres) of the most beautiful part of Co Donegal, with magnificent lakeside views from Glenveagh Castle. Nearby is **Glebe House and Gallery** (charge; http://glebegallery.ie), an elegant Regency country house and gardens built in 1828. This was once the home of the artist Derek Hill, who bequeathed it along with his art collection to the Irish state in 1981.

NORTHERN IRELAND

HIGHLIGHTS

- Belfast, see page 92
- The Antrim Coast Road, see page 95
- Derry City and Fermanagh, see page 97
- Mountains of Mourne, see page 99

Although a troubled region throughout much of the twentieth century, it's become hard to be sure of the exact location of the border between the Republic and Northern Ireland since the 1998 Good Friday Agreement led to a lessening of violence and the removal of army checkpoints. The border – a hot topic in the UK's Brexit negotiations – snakes its way along eighteenth-century county boundaries, through farming land that is sometimes bleak, more often breathtakingly beautiful, and takes little account of natural boundaries such as rivers, or of the cultural differences that separate Republican-minded Roman Catholics and Unionist-oriented Protestants. Houses straddle it so that, as the joke has it, a man may sleep with his head in the United Kingdom and his heart in the Republic of Ireland.

Political expediency accounts for the absurdities. The intention was to redraw the border rationally after partition in 1920 left six

The Hands Across the Divide statue in Derry

of the nine counties of the ancient province of Ulster (Antrim, Down, Armagh, Derry, Fermanagh and Tyrone) under British rule, and a Boundary Commission was set up. But in the end the British and Irish governments, both hoping to avoid further trouble, suppressed the commission's report and left things as they were.

BELFAST

Belfast ㊴, the capital, looks little different from a provincial English city. **Donegall Place** is lined with UK chain stores, while post boxes are no longer green, as in the Republic, but red. Sectarian tensions are, by and large, a thing of the past: nowadays bus and taxi tours show visitors where the worst riots of the 1970s and 1980s took place.

Queen's University, Belfast

Set in a saucer of green hills and spanning the mouth of the River Lagan as it flows into the Irish Sea, Belfast is essentially a Victorian creation, its wealth founded on textile manufacturing and shipbuilding. Today most of the factories have vanished, though two towering yellow cranes (Samson and Goliath) survive as a reminder of the great days of Harland & Wolff shipyard, birthplace of the *Titanic*.

Titanic Belfast

Dominating the centre in Donegall Square is the 1906 **City Hall** Ⓐ the architecture of which has been dubbed 'Wrenaissance', in tribute to its shameless resemblance to Sir Christopher Wren's St Paul's Cathedral in London. Queen Victoria presides over the area outside, her statue supported by workers from the linen and shipbuilding industries. Inside, an ornate marble staircase sweeps up to the Rotunda, and the banqueting hall and council chamber are suitably extravagant. Free guided **tours** show visitors around the building, but more illuminating is the ground floor exhibition, which charts the city's history courtesy of sixteen differently themed rooms

To the north of the City Hall, Donegall Place, which becomes Royal Avenue, is Belfast's main shopping thoroughfare. **Linen Hall Library** Ⓑ, on Donegall Square North, is a revered public-subscription library – a treasure house for historians and political journalists. Close by, on Great Victoria Street, are two architectural gems:

the 1895 **Grand Opera House** Ⓒ (www.goh.co.uk), with its plush brass and velvet, its gilded elephant heads and excellent acoustics, and the **Crown Liquor Saloon** Ⓓ, a riot of Victorian Baroque, owned by the National Trust but still serving the finest Guinness and whisky.

Great Victoria Street leads on, via Shaftesbury Square, to the Tudor-style **Queen's University** Ⓔ, whose central tower bears a suspicious resemblance to that of Magdalen College, Oxford. The university has colonised just about every available building in the vicinity, but welcome green space is provided by the adjacent **Royal Botanic Gardens** Ⓕ, which contain a curvilinear Palm House. Beside the park is the revamped **Ulster Museum** Ⓖ (free; http://ulstermuseum.org) whose clever design sheds light both

The Giant's Causeway

literally and figuratively on subjects ranging from the North's troubled history to Ireland's geological past.

Belfast, of course, has many churches. Chief among them are the neo-Romanesque **St Anne's Cathedral** H in Donegall Street, the extravagantly decorated interior of **St Malachy's Church** I in Clarence Street and the delightful **First Presbyterian Church** J in Rosemary Street.

Across the River Lagan, in the newly named Titanic Quarter, at the heart of which is **Titanic Belfast** K (charge; www.titanicbelfast.com), the world's largest Titanic visitor experience. Inside are a series of well thought out galleries variously pertaining to the city's industrial past, the history of Harland and Wolff and the construction of *Titanic*, and, ultimately, its fateful journey.

Close by is the **SSE Arena** L (www.ssearenabelfast.com), a venue for sporting events and pop concerts, and the **W5** (times vary; www.w5online.co.uk) science and discovery centre.

In nearby Alexandra Dock stands HMS Caroline (charge; http://nmrn.org.uk), a World War One light cruiser and the sole survivor from the 1916 Battle of Jutland.

THE ANTRIM COAST ROAD

To the northeast of Belfast, past Carrickfergus (which has a fine Norman castle) and the industrial port of **Larne** 40, the lovely **Antrim Coast Road** runs alongside the Irish Sea through picturesque villages such as **Cushendall** and **Cushendun**. Diversions can be made along the way into any of the nine green glens, peaceful landscapes traditionally farmed.

The north coast begins at **Ballycastle** 41, setting for the Ould Lammas Fair (an agricultural fair held in August since 1606), and the ferry departure point for a 13km (8 mile) trip to Rathlin Island, whose population of around 140 is vastly outnumbered by seabirds. Continuing east, you pass Carrick-a-Rede Rope Bridge (charge; www.nationaltrust.org.uk/carrick-a-rede), which swings over a 24-m

The Guildhall Clocktower, Derry

(80-ft) chasm, allowing salmon fishermen and brave tourists access to a rocky promontory. Past cliffs and white surfers' beaches are the romantic ruins of the sixth-century Dunseverick Castle.

Bushmills is home to the world's oldest distillery (charge; www.bushmills.eu), where can learn about the process on a guided **tour,** which takes in the mash house, the malt barn, the vast warehouse, and the equally impressive bottling plant; the tour ends with a complimentary tasting.

It is also the jumping-off point for Ireland's most spectacular natural phenomenon, the **Giant's Causeway** ㊷ (charge; www.nationaltrust.org.uk/giants-causeway). Formed 60 million years ago when molten lava froze into 38,000 basalt columns, mostly hexagonal, it looks like a series of giant stepping-stones. Park near the visitor centre or, in season, catch a narrow-gauge steam locomotive from

Bushmills. To the west are the resorts of Portrush and **Portstewart**, and the ruins of the fourteenth-century **Dunluce Castle**.

DERRY CITY AND FERMANAGH

Protestants still call **Derry** ㊸, Northern Ireland's second city, Londonderry, the name given to it by the London guilds who began creating the walled city in 1614 – its 6m- (20ft-) thick walls boast watchtowers and cannons, such as the 1642 'Roaring Meg'. The excellent **Tower Museum** (charge; http://towermuseumcollections.com), in Union Hall Place, relates the city's troubled history in lucid fashion. **St Columb's Cathedral**, occupying the south-western corner of the walled city, is a graceful seventeenth-century Anglican church, and whose **chapterhouse museum** holds the padlocks and keys used to lock the city gates.

3.5km (5 miles) north of Omagh is The **Ulster American Folk Park** ㊹ (free; http://ulsteramericanfolkpark.org), where rebuilt craftsmen's cottages, a schoolhouse and forge recreate

MUSIC AND MURALS

Northern Ireland's popular culture portrays the sectarian divide with the bluntness of bombs and bullets. Triumphalist or threatening murals adorn the sides of hundreds of houses, particularly in Belfast and Derry. The Protestant versions often feature William of Orange, who defeated his Catholic father-in-law, James II, at the Battle of the Boyne in 1690. Catholic murals celebrate Republican heroes and aspirations, while balaclava-clad men brandishing rifles are common to both traditions. The worst murals are crudely executed; the best can be viewed as exceptional folk art.

For both Protestants and Catholics, marching bands keep history alive and mark out territory. The biggest parades are staged on 12 July by Protestant Orangemen (commemorating William of Orange). On the surface it's tuneful pageantry – but it can also be fiercely provocative.

eighteenth-century living conditions here. Meanwhile, log cabins and covered wagons illustrate the New World that many emigrants created in America; it is said that 11 US presidents had their roots in the province.

Further south, Fermanagh is the province's lakeland playground. Summer pleasure boats ply the lakes from the busy county town of **Enniskillen** ㊺. On Lower Lough Erne, **Boa Island** has an ancient two-faced Janus statue and **Devenish Island** has a fine round tower.

Heading back towards the east coast, **Armagh** ㊻ has two fine cathedrals (both called St Patrick's), some notable Georgian buildings and a planetarium. Just outside the town is Navan Fort, one of Ireland's most important historical sites – the ancient seat of the kings of Ulster.

The mighty Mourne Mountains

MOUNTAINS OF MOURNE

Close to the Irish Sea, the fifteen granite peaks of the **Mourne Mountains** ❹❼ reach to more than 600m (2,000ft). You can hike to the summit of Slieve Donard, starting at Donard Park (taking five to six hours round trip; check the forecast first). At the top are two cairns (ancient mounds of stones) – from here, on a clear day, you can see Scotland, England, the Isle of Man, and Snowdonia in Wales.

Ulster Folk Museum

Passing through Downpatrick, you can take the ferry from Strangford to Portaferry and drive up the **Ards Peninsula** ❹❽, a 37km- (23 mile-), a long finger dotted by villages and beaches. Mount Stewart, an eighteenth-century mansion, has one of Europe's greatest gardens; among others, there are **Spanish** and **Italian** gardens, a **Sunk Garden**, and the **Shamrock Garden**.

At Cultra, near Holywood on the main road into Belfast, the **Ulster Folk Museum and Ulster Transport Museums** ❹❾ (free; http://ulsterfolkmuseum.org and http://ulstertransportmuseum.org) are set in 70 hectares (170 acres) of a green and picnic-friendly woodland park; the former is an open-air **village** with about thirty typical buildings from all over the North, some dating from the eighteenth century, while the latter packs in every conceivable form of transport, from horse-drawn carts to lifeboats and even a vertical take-off plane.

Walking in the Mourne Mountains

Things to do

OUTDOOR ACTIVITIES

Despite the weather, Ireland is a great place for getting out and about. Cycling is one of the best ways to appreciate the quiet pleasures of the Irish countryside, while walkers can take advantage of generally free access across much of the countryside and a number of waymarked trails. With over 120 sailing and yacht clubs, plenty of lakes, rivers and sheltered coastline to explore and some great beaches for surfers, there are many opportunities for watersports enthusiasts, too.

In terms of spectator sports, hurling and Gaelic football are among the fastest and most physical sports in the world, and well worth catching on your travels, whether on TV or, preferably, live. Rugby and soccer are also widely followed, while going to the races is a great day out, with less of the snobbery sometimes found in Britain. Golf is also hugely popular north and south of the border.

Cycling Signposted cycling trails in the Republic include the Beara Way and the Sheep's Head Cycling Route in Cork, and the Kerry Way. On- and off-road routes are detailed on http://sportireland.ie, but trails in the North are better documented and promoted: for detailed information on the many routes here, the best places to start are http://cycleni.com and http://sustrans.org.uk. They include the Kingfisher Trail, which also stretches into Leitrim and Cavan. Other cross-border routes include the 326km North West Trail, mainly on quiet country roads through Donegal, Tyrone, Fermanagh, Leitrim and Sligo.

Walking There are dozens of waymarked long-distance walking trails in the Republic, ranging from routes through or around mountain ranges, such as the Wicklow Way, the Táin Way, the Slieve Bloom Way and the Western Way, to walks around entire peninsulas, like the Sheep's Head Way, the Beara Way, the Kerry Way and the Dingle Way. The Ulster Way in the North, the oldest and longest waymarked walking trail in Ireland, is a 625-mile circuit of the whole province, taking in the Giant's Causeway, the Sperrins and the Mournes; it's now divided into link sections, which can be skipped by taking public transport, and quality sections. For information on these trails in the Republic, go to http://sportireland.ie, which also has details of hundreds of looped day walks. In the North, http://walkni.com has comprehensive information on all aspects of walking.

Golf Golf was probably first brought to Ireland by the Ulster Scots, and the sport attracts huge numbers of visitors every year,. Indeed, thanks to the likes of Rory McIlroy (from Holywood, near Belfast) and Shane Lowry (form Clara in Co. Offaly), the game has never been more popular. Golf in Ireland has also received a massive boost in recent years thanks to the staging of the Open Championship at Portrush in Northern Ireland, with the next one in 2025. The Golfing Union of Ireland, based in Kildare (http://golfnet.ie), provides details of over four hundred clubs, north and south, with online booking.

Horse riding Whether over the hills or along the beaches, is also a popular pastime, for both novices and experienced riders, who also have the option of multi-day trails rides. Stables in popular locations are listed throughout the Guide, including Killarney and Clifden. The Association of Irish Riding Establishments (http://aire.ie) maintains standards among riding centres in the Republic and the North and publishes details on its website (http://discovernorthernireland.com).

Fishing There are plenty of opportunities for sea angling and dozens of rivers and lakes for fly- and game-fishing. For information, the best places to start are Angling Ireland's website, http://fishinginireland.info, and the tourist-board site, http://ireland.com. Great Fishing Houses of Ireland (http://irelandflyfishing.com) covers a dozen or so specialist hotels and B&Bs.

Riding ponies on Cleggan Beach in Connemara

Horse racing. Almost everyone in Ireland seems to be totally engrossed, one way or another, in the sport of kings. The main courses are the Curragh and Punchestown, both in Co. Kildare, and Fairyhouse in Co. Meath. The flat season is from March to November, and steeplechasing goes on all year. See www.go racing.ie for information on events.

Hurling and Gaelic football. Hurling, which has been played for 4,000 years, is a very fast and exciting high-scoring game where a small, leather ball (*sliotar*) is struck with a wooden hurley (like hockey but at head height). Gaelic football, Ireland's other traditional sport, ostensibly resembles a marriage between soccer and rugby and entails the use of a Gaelic ball (slightly smaller than a soccer ball), which can be both kicked and caught. For more information on Gaelic sporting events and the history of the sports, visit www.gaa.ie.

WATERSPORTS

Canoeing and kayaking Inland waterways and sheltered coasts – notably in west Cork, Dingle and Waterford – offer canoeing and kayaking opportunities, ranging from day-trips and touring to rough- and white-water racing. Canoeing Ireland's website covers courses and clubs in the South (http://canoe.ie), while the North has a comprehensive website, http://canoeni.com, that includes canoe trails for multi-day touring. Another useful website is http://iska.ie.

Sailing The most popular areas for sailing are the relatively sheltered waters of the east coast, especially in Dublin Bay; Cork Harbour and west Cork. Look out, too, ofr the many regattas taking place. See www.sailing.ie.

Scuba diving Right in the path of the warm North Atlantic Drift current, Ireland offers some of the best scuba diving in Europe, notably off the rocky west coast Along the north coast there are lots of wreck dives, with Spanish galleons from the Armada resting beneath the waves. See www.scuba.ie and http://diving.ie

Swimming Blue Flag beaches have to meet certain safety criteria, including having adequate life-saving equipment and, if necessary, lifeguards on duty and beautiful beaches can be found all along the country's coastline. For a list of Blue Flag beaches all over Ireland, visit www.beachawards.ie/blue-flag.

Surfing, wind-surfing and kite-surfing The heavy Atlantic swells are more impressive on the west coast, where the biggest surfing bases are Lahinch Co Clare, Strandhill Co Sligo, Bundoran Co Donegal, and Tramore Co Waterford, on the east coast. See www.irishsurfing.ie, www.windsurfing.ie and www.kitesurfingireland.ie

SHOPPING

Friendly sales staff make shopping in Ireland a real pleasure. The most appealing products are made by Irish craftsmen in traditional or new styles; the Kilkenny Design Centre in Kilkenny City has a particularly fine range of traditional goods on offer. The Design and Crafts

Council's website at www.dcci.ie is also a good starting point that enables you to research what's available in the area you're visiting.

For clothes or slightly more eclectic souvenirs, Dublin is the place to visit, with everything from upscale boutiques to huge shopping malls: check out the vast **Dundrum Town Centre** (www.dundrum.ie), just outside Dublin city centre, or the more intimate **Powerscourt Centre** (www.powerscourtcentre.ie). **Grafton Street** is the main shopping street, with high street names and fashionable department stores such as the much-loved Brown Thomas (www.brownthomas.com). Other interesting shops include the **House of Names** (www.houseofnames.ie), Nassau Street, whose handmade coats of arms allegedly feature the crests of more than 96 percent of the world's surnames; and **George's Street Arcade** (www.georgesstreetarcade.ie), just off South Great George's, a vibrant indoor market with an eclectic worldwide mix of goods, from Greek olives to Peruvian handwoven rugs.

Bodhráns or traditional drums

WHAT TO BUY

Aran jumpers. Demand so far exceeds supply that they are now made in mainland factories as well as on the Aran islands. For genuinely hand-knitted jumpers, go to Blarney Woollen Mills (www.blarney.com) in Cork, Ó'Máille (www.omaille.com) in Galway and Cleo Ltd (www.cleo-ltd.com) in Dublin.

Connemara marble. A rich green, this stone is unique to Ireland. All sorts of souvenirs are made from Connemara marble, especially jewellery.

Chocolate. Buy delicious hand-made chocolates at Butler's Chocolates in Grafton Street, Dublin, and at the Skelligs Chocolate Factory in Ballinskelligs, Co Kerry. Try before you buy at the Lir Cafés in Killarney, Co Kerry.

Metal working. Enamel bowls, plaques, and pendants by master craftspeople.

Crosses. Reproductions of old Christian crosses and St Brigid crosses made out of straw.

Toys. In Dublin, Avoca (www.avoca.com) and Arnotts (www.arnotts.ie) both have extensive toy departments. Other favourites are Bumblebee Creations (www.bumblebeecreations.ie – check out their kids' hurling kit, the 'Hurlóg') and craft creations from Little Green Dot (www.greendotdesignshop.com).

Glassware. Waterford crystal (www.waterford.com) is world renowned, while Jerpoint Glass (www.jerpointglass.com) in County Kilkenny produces hand-blown uncut crystal in contemporary designs.

Jewellery. Celtic designs inspire many of today's goldsmiths and silversmiths, while others work in a contemporary style. In Dublin, head to DesignYard (www.designyard.com) for high-end Irish jewellery.

Lace. Although a waning trade in Limerick and Co Monaghan, there is now a strong revival of lacemaking in Carrickmacross, Clones, Kenmare, and Youghal.

Linen. Weaving continues in Northern Ireland, with a huge emphasis on quality. Irish Linen should bear the Irish Linen Guild's trademark, see www.irishlinen.co.uk. Brands such as Thomas Ferguson and Baird McNutt are heirloom quality.

Musical instruments. Bodhráns, flutes, tin whistles, there's many suitcase-friendly musical instruments widely available.

Master craftsman at work

Paintings. Artists produce fine studies of Ireland, including landscapes, seascapes, flora and fauna, in oils, watercolours, prints, and etchings. Check out Merrion Square (www.merrionart.com) in Dublin.

Peat. Even the turf of Ireland is compressed and sculpted to reproduce ancient religious and folklore symbols.

Pottery. Traditional and modern designs, sought after by collectors. Louis Mulcahy in Ballyferriter, Co Kenny, and Nicholas Mosse Pottery from Co Kilkenny are always in fashion.

Rushwork. In a land rich in thatched cottages, the makers of woven baskets and similar wickerwork still thrive.

Smoked salmon. Specially packed for travelling, and on sale at the airport. Opt for wild salmon that is certified organic.

Souvenirs. Leprechauns, marble worry stones, and *shillelaghs* (short wooden clubs) are all widely available. Books about Irish history make easy-to-carry souvenirs. GAA jerseys are a quirky gift – wear your county colours with pride!

Tweed and Wool. Handwoven fabrics in a variety of colours and weights, traditionally weaved in Donegal. Check out Magee (www.magee1866.com) on Wicklow St, Dublin and McNutt of Donegal in the Gaeltacht village of Downings, Co Donegal.

Wood turning. Many wood turners use only storm-damaged timber, making an ecologically sound product.

CULTURE

TRADITIONAL MUSIC

Many hotels and pubs provide entertainment, featuring a diverse cross-section of traditional Irish entertainment: folk singers, harpists, dancers, and storytellers. In local pubs 'trad' (traditional) sessions can break out at any moment, with singers and musicians joining in. At the other end of the scale, luxury hotels put on elaborate productions. The shows have a typically Irish mixture of hand-clapping high spirits and 'Come Back to Erin' nostalgia. Jigs and reels are tirelessly danced, and lively tap dancers revive some of the country's oldest and best routines. *Bodhrans* (Irish drums), banjos, bagpipes, and accordions are all played with gusto, and fast fiddlers are ubiquitous.

You will find more genuine versions of traditional Irish music at *fleadhanna*, festivals of music and song around the island, climaxing in the All Ireland *Fleadh* in August. Tourist offices will have detailed schedules of such events (www.fleadhnua.com).

PUBS, BARS AND CLUBS

The traditional pub is the heartbeat of Irish life and you can still find the real thing all over the country. Dubliners boast that their city possesses the finest **pubs** in the world, and they may well be right. And with over seven hundred watering holes to choose from, forming the backbone of the capital's social life, there's no harm in checking out their assertion. Along the way, you'll also be able to test out competing claims about the hometown drink, **Guinness**. Alongside the more traditional pubs, a plethora of cosmopolitan **bars** has sprung up, be they cavernous microbreweries serving craft beers, studenty DJ bars or chic designer cocktail lounges. Traditional music pubs are great for a drink in their own right. Dublin also has a number of LGBTQ bars as well as some highly entertaining pub tours.

Trad music session in a local pub

THEATRE

Ireland's grand theatrical tradition – which gave the world Goldsmith, Shaw, Sheridan, Beckett, O'Casey, and more recently Conor McPherson and Martin McDonagh – continues in major towns such as Dublin, Belfast, and Cork. Tickets are usually available on the night at Ireland's National Theatre, the Abbey Theatre (www.abbeytheatre.ie) and the Gate Theatre (www.gatetheatre.ie) in Dublin. See www.entertainment.ie for full listings of concerts, theatre, and film.

LITERATURE

For an island of fewer than six million people, Ireland has an astonishingly rich literary tradition. This is a tradition that has developed over two thousand years from the first markings on rocks around the time of Christ, to the acclaimed poetry, prose and theatre of

TradFest in Temple Bar

writers such as W.B. Yeats, James Joyce and Samuel Beckett, producing startling works of originality and influence.

FESTIVALS AND EVENTS

Ireland has a plethora of annual festivals, ranging from small local affairs to major international occasions and significant events in the sporting calendar.

January: *TradFest Temple Bar*, Dublin – traditional and folk music festival; *Shannonside Winter Music Weekend*, Co Clare – acoustic music festival.

February: *Dublin International Film Festival.*

March: *St Patrick's Week* – celebrations throughout Ireland; *Killarney Mountain Festival* – outdoor sport and adventure; *Tedfest, Aran Islands* – lots of wacky events in homage to the popular sitcom.

April: *Pan-Celtic International Festival*, Co Carlow – music, song, dance, and cultural events; *Irish Grand National Weekend at Fairyhouse*, Co Meath; *Waterford Festival of Food*.

May: *The Cork International Choral Festival; Fleadh Nua* – traditional music and dance in Ennis, Co Clare; *Slieve Bloom Walking Festival*, Kinnitty, Co Offaly; *The Cat Laughs Comedy Festival*, Kilkenny.

June: *Listowel Writers Week*, Co Kerry; *Bloomsday*, celebration of James Joyce on the day his novel Ulysses is set, Dublin; *Great Music in Irish Houses Chamber Music Festival*, all over Ireland; *Cork Midsummer Festival* – huge arts festival; *SeaFest*, Cork; *Irish Derby*, Curragh racecourse, Co Kildare.

July: *Galway Races; Galway International Arts Festival; Lady of the Lake Festival*, Enniskillen, Co Fermanagh; *Earagail Arts Festival* – music and arts festival, Co Donegal.

August: *Connemara Pony Show*, Clifden, Co Galway; *Kilkenny Arts Festival; Oul' Lammas Fair*, Ballycastle, Co Antrim; *Puck Fair* – parades and family fun in Killorglin, Co Kerry; *Stradbally Steam Rally*, Co Laois; *Rose of Tralee International Festival, Kerry*

September: *GAA All-Ireland Senior Hurling Final*, Dublin; *Clarenbridge Oyster Festival*, Galway; *Dublin Theatre Festival; Lisdoonvarna Matchmaking Festival*, Co Clare – traditional matchmaking amid much merriment.

October: *Kinsale Gourmet Festival*, Co Cork; *Bram Stoker Festival*, Dublin; *Ballinasloe Fair*, Co Galway – Europe's oldest horse fair; *Cork Jazz Festival*; Wexford Opera Festival; *Belfast International Arts Festival*. Major arts festival.

November: *Cork International Film Festival*; *National Circus Festival Ireland*, Tralee, Co Kerry – watch and learn circus skills; *Dublin Book Festival* – readings, workshops and literary walking tours.

December: *Glow – a Cork Christmas Celebration; Leopardstown Christmas Festival; Limerick Christmas Racing Festival; Guinness Choir Christmas Concert*, St Patrick's Cathedral, Dublin. *Wonderlights* (venue changes annually).

Food and drink

Historically, few visitors have come to Ireland just for the food (though plenty come to drink), but the quality and choice on offer has improved markedly in the last decade or so. A new generation of small-scale artisan producers has emerged, be they cheese-makers, organic farmers, fish-smokers or bakers, and the best Irish chefs seek out this local produce to re-create and adapt traditional dishes using global techniques.

It's well worth looking out for Good Food Ireland signs (or checking out http://goodfoodireland.ie), a network of high-quality restaurants, cafés, hotels, producers and cookery schools, who are committed to using local, seasonal, artisan ingredients wherever possible.

Galway Bay oysters

TOP 10 THINGS TO TRY

1. GALWAY OYSTERS

These large, silky European flat oysters are some of the best in the world, having matured for about three years in anticipation of a season that runs from September until April.

2. CHEESE

Since the 1970s, cheese-making has blossomed once again, especially in Munster, often handmade by farmers; try Desmond, a piquant, long-matured, Swiss-style cheese from Co. Cork, and Wicklow Ban, a mild and creamy Brie hand-crafted on a family farm in Wicklow.

NOTES

You don't have to look far to find an idyllic setting for a picnic in Ireland. Farmhouse cheeses, smoked salmon, freshly baked bread and seasonal produce supply the ingredients. As for the setting, chose from the dramatic winding coastline, romantic forest parks or moody mountain views. The only thing that can't be guaranteed is the weather.

3. GUINNESS

A dark, creamy stout that has long been Ireland's most popular drink. Guinness is the market leader, but Beamish and Murphy's from Cork are also worth trying.

4. LAMB

Variants to look out for include Achill lamb – as the animals graze on seaside meadows, the meat is naturally salty and a little sweet; and air-dried Connemara lamb from Oughterard, a little like Italian Parma ham.

5. BLACK AND WHITE PUDDING

Usually part of a cooked Irish breakfast, this is a sausage of pig's blood; white pudding is made from pig's offal and cereals – you'll either love it or hate it.

Lamb shank

6. COLCANNON

Popular dish of mashed potato mixed with cabbage and often leeks. The Northern Irish version is called champ, but flavoured with spring onions.

7. IRISH STEW

A filling casserole of meat, potatoes, carrots and onions, laced with parsley and thyme.

8. SODA BREAD

Bread baked with bicarbonate of soda, buttermilk and flour; simple but delicious, especially when spread liberally with butter.

9. BARMBRACK

A fruity tea loaf smothered in butter, it's best eaten with a cup of tea in the afternoon.

10. CODDLE

A working-class Dublin dish, the name coddle comes from the slow simmering or 'coddling' of ingredients in a one-pot stew – slices of pork sausage packed in alongside bacon rashers or boiled bacon and sliced potatoes and onions.

WHERE TO EAT

The widest array of restaurants is concentrated in the big cities – where, alongside Dublin and Belfast, Cork has a particularly vibrant scene – and in gourmet hotspots such as Kilkenny, Kinsale, Kenmare and Dingle, but good places can be found all over the country, sometimes in quite unexpected locales. Between them, the Republic and Northern Ireland now have a remarkable twenty Michelin-starred restaurants, a handful of which are in Dublin. There are also an increasing number of dedicated vegetarian and vegan restaurants – which are far more preferable to the token dishes offered in many pubs and restaurants.

Most pubs across the country will be able to rustle you up a simple lunch, typically sandwiches and salads – which regularly feature crab and other seafood in coastal areas – and hot staples such as Irish stew and soups. But while occasionally the offerings can be dull, Ireland's foodie renaissance, and a commercial need to diversify, means that many have had to up their game. Similar fare is also available in traditional daytime cafés, alongside cakes and scones, which are now augmented in some towns by deli-cafés, offering a more interesting array of food.

Black pudding

Virtually every sizeable town now hosts a farmers' market, often on a Saturday. The best markets – colourful, vibrant affairs that are worth a visit in their own right – are the permanent English Market in Cork city; the Temple Bar Food Market in Dublin, the Galway city market and the Midleton

The Pig's Back, English Market, Cork

market in east Cork, all on Saturdays; and St George's Market in Belfast, on Fridays and Saturdays.

WHEN TO EAT

Breakfast is served from about 7–10am, though in some hotels, it might not begin until 8am, at least at weekends. Lunchtime is from 12.30–2.30pm, give or take half an hour at either end. It's worth noting that many fine restaurants offer cheaper, simpler menus at lunch time, and plenty also lay on good-value early-bird menus in the evening – two or three courses for a set price, usually available until 7 or 7.30pm, though often not at weekends. The time of the evening meal depends on where you are. In rural areas and perhaps the less sophisticated town areas, people dine as early as 6pm. In the major towns and cities, however, you can eat any time from 6 or 7–10pm.

Places to eat

To give you an idea of prices, we have used the following symbols for a three-course meal for one excluding wine:

€€€ over €40
€€ €20–40
€ under €20
£££ over £35
££ £15–35
£ under £15

DUBLIN

Chapter One Restaurant 18/19 Parnell Square, Dublin 1, www.chapteronerestaurant.com. Housed in the cellars of the former Dublin Writers Museum, this two-starred Michelin-starred culinary gem is Dublin's big ticket restaurant. Specializing in modern Irish food, inspired by the Irish landscape, seasons and new Irish artisan producers, the three menus (Lunch, Dinner, Tasting; €85–190) might include the likes of pig's tail stuffed with Fingal Ferguson's bacon or roast Anjou pigeon, *Céret* cherries and liver ganache. Book weeks, if not months, in advance. Closed Sun–Tues. **€€€€**

Cornucopia 19 Wicklow Street, Dublin 2, www.cornucopia.ie. Friendly, vegetarian/vegan, buffet café serving an excellent range of breakfasts, salads, soups and main courses, as well as cakes, breads, juices and organic wine. **€**

Ely Winebar 22 Ely Place, St Stephen's Green, Dublin 2, www.elywinebar.ie. Popular, congenial and reasonably- priced wine bar that offers snacks and main meals like pan-fried guinea fowl with barley and bacon, to accompany around eighty wines by the glass. Carefully sourced, mostly organic Irish ingredients, including fresh beef and pork from their own farm in the Burren. Closed Sun. **€€€**

Fallon & Byrne 11-17 Exchequer Street, Dublin 2, www.fallonandbyrne.com. Foodie heaven in a converted telephone exchange: a smart grocery store and deli (for lunch to eat in or take away) on the ground floor; a seductive, Parisian-style brasserie upstairs, offering everything from burgers to superb seared sea bream with squid terrine and smoked almond oil; and a wine bar and shop in the basement, serving cheaper food. **€–€€**

Sano Pizza 1–2 Exchange Street Upper, http://sano.pizza.ie. As a sign of how expensive it can be to eat in Dublin, you'll do well to find a decent pizza anywhere for much less than €15, but Sano bucks that trend, and in some style; deliciously doughy pizzas served quickly and cheaply, and some decent vegan options too. Great stuff. **€€**

Wuff 23 Benburb St, http://wuffrestaurant.ie. A lively neighbourhood bistro in the heart of Smithfield, serving up the likes of veggie chorizo benedict breakfast, pulled jackfruit sandwiches and salads for lunch, and heartier dishes like golden beer-battered fish with twice-cooked chips for dinner. **€€**

CORK

Ballymaloe House Shanagarry, www.ballymaloe.ie. This stalwart on Ireland's fine dining scene, made famous by chef Darina Allen, offers exceptional modern dishes using local ingredients, such as housemade fettuccine with basil pesto, and Cloyne beef cheek ragout with Garryhinch mushrooms and roast parsnips, while you choose your dessert from a groaning trolley. **€€€**

Farmgate Café English Market, Princes St, http://farmgate.ie. Superb café-restaurant overlooking the market's bustling stalls. Places a strong emphasis on local ingredients and food products: daily specials depend on what's fresh from the butcher and fishmonger. Cooked breakfasts to order, great cakes and desserts and excellent lunches, which feature salads and savoury tarts, as well as many classic dishes such as tripe and onion with drisheen. **€€**

Market Lane 5 Oliver Plunkett St, http://marketlane.ie. Crisp bistro decor featuring lots of polished wood, an open kitchen and a long bar in a bright corner location provides the setting for some outstandingly creative dishes like pan fried hake with sweet potato and coconut gratin and crispy buckwheat, and, for vegans, dal vada lentil cakes with cashew yoghurt and sweet pickled cucumber. Good value set lunch menus. **€€€**

GALWAY

Ard Bia at Nimmo's Spanish Arch, Galway City, www.ardbia.com. Set in a stone-built medieval customs house by the river, with rustic-chic decor, and modern art on the walls. The perfectly paced modern Irish food focuses on expertly prepared local, seasonal ingredients, with a few Middle Eastern touches. Lunch includes beef and harissa *shaksuka*, with a dinner menu comprising the likes of monkfish, spiced cauliflower and chermoula. **€€**

McDonagh's Seafood House 22 Quay Street, Galway City www.mcdonaghs.net. This Galway institution features nautical paraphernalia and a menu that casts its net wide: pan-fried mackerel, baked monkfish, lemon sole, red gurnard, grilled ray, wild Clarinbridge oysters, and scallops are all on offer, as are good old fashioned fish and chips – Galway's finest? **€–€€**

Moran's Oyster Cottage The Weir, Kilcolgan, http://moransoystercottage.com. A bar and restaurant set by the bay and famed for native oysters (from their own beds) accompanied by brown bread and a creamy pint of stout. Seafood platters, crab claws, mussels or Aran Islands prawns are all available as well as vegetarian lasagne. Closed Mon. **€–€€**

Upstairs @ McCambridge's Shop St, http://mccambridges.com. A wonderful addition to the Galwegian culinary scene, above a deli that has been in business since 1925. Prepare to indulge yourself in the all-day menu featuring cold platters of cheese, meat or seafood, salads, frittatas, and hot dishes such as lamb kebabs or roasted prawns. Closed Sun. **€–€€**

KERRY

Ashe's Main St, Dingle http://ashesrestaurant.ie. Easygoing spot, more restaurant than pub, which specializes in stunningly creative seafood dishes such as crab and prawn dumplings, and roasted spiced scallops with homemade mango chutney and cumin yoghurt. The bar, too, is a terrific spot to down a cocktail. Closed Sun & Mon. **€€**

Bricin Restaurant 26 High Street, Killarney, www.bricin.ie. Homely restaurant that serves traditional Irish food, notably filled boxties (potato pancakes), as well as more eclectic dishes such as Thai red chicken curry with jasmine rice in a coconut milk sauce; commendably, there's also a dedicated vegan menu. **€€**

Harrow 27 High St, Kenmare http://harrowkillarney.com. Stylish brasserie – formal but far from stuffy – with a predominantly beef and seafood menu (featherblade with malt glazed carrot smoked potato puree and dried onion crumble), though there are also one or two startlingly good vegan dishes, like shallot tarte tatin with celeriac confit and walnut oil. Closed Mon–Wed. **€€€**

Mulcahy's 16 Main St, Kenmare http://mulcahyskenmare.ie. Crisp, modern decor is the setting for excellent creative cuisine with global (largely French) influences. Expect dishes such as chicken and sneem black pudding *boudain*, and halibut grape and leek *beurre blanc*. Closed Sun & Mon. **€€€**

LIMERICK AND SHANNON

1826 Adare Main St, Adare http://1826adare.ie. The focus of this chic restaurant, set in a delightful row of thatched cottages, is on keenly priced casual dining. Their signature dish is the free-range pork tasting plate of loin belly cheek and black pudding, but you'll also find blackboard specials such as sole and braised meats. **€€**

Cornstore Restaurant Thomas St, Limerick http://cornstore.ie. Covering three floors and incorporating a wine and cocktail bar, the lively *Cornstore* specializes in seafood such as seared tuna steak with olive tapenade and garlic potato cream, and dry-aged steaks including chateaubriand to share for two. An à la carte menu is complemented by very reasonably priced set menus costing €40 and €50. **€€€**

House Howley's Quay, Limerick http://houselimerick.ie. Watch the swans preening in the Shannon as you dine al fresco at this elegant quayside restaurant with meat (buttermilk chicken with chipotle mayo; chargrilled steaks) and fish (Atlantic prawn Pil Pil with Gubbeen chorizo) forming the mainstay of the all-day menu, although veggies and vegans are taken care of too (vegan cauliflower wings with smoked paprika). **€€**

The Mustard Seed at Echo Lodge Newcastle West Road, Ballingarry, www.mustardseed.ie. Set in a country residence, this is one of the country's foremost restaurants, with an inspired modern Irish menu drawing from the produce of its organic garden. The four-course "classic" dinner (€72) is served nightly; main courses typically include rib-eye of beef, monkfish and guinea fowl. **€€€**

WATERFORD

Cliff House Hotel Ardmore, Co Waterford, www.cliffhousehotel.ie. "McGrath's Black Angus Beef: Garden Spinach, Potato, Kilbeggan Whiskey,

Beef Tea"... the menu entries at this superb Michelin-starred restaurant in a stunning location overlooking the sea run on like a Joycean stream of consciousness. There's plenty of imagination, too, in the complex but supremely skilful combinations of unusual ingredients, and in their intricate, almost sculptural, platings. **€€€**

The Strand Inn 7 Wellington Terrace, Dunmore East, Co Waterford, www.thestrandinn.com. Situated beside a former smuggler's cove, this three hundred-year-old inn specializes in fresh seafood, in dishes such as spicy and hot devilled crab "au gratin", steaks, pastas and burgers, with plentiful outdoor tables overlooking the beach. Children's menu available, too with generous portions. **€–€€**

The Tannery Restaurant 10 Quay Street, Dungarvan, www.tannery.ie. Excellent modern Irish restaurant in a stylishly converted leather warehouse, owned by TV chef Paul Flynn, who also offers cookery courses. Local, seasonal ingredients are used wherever possible in dishes such as crab *crème brûlée*, and duck breast with potato terrine and salt baked celeriac. **€€€**

WEXFORD

Green Acres Selskar Street, Wexford, www.greenacres.ie. A handsome redbrick house with a modern glass extension. Inside you'll find a well-stocked deli and wine shop, a first-floor art gallery and a bistro serving creative fare such as wild Wicklow game pie with braised kale and pickled cranberries. **€€**

The Wilds 23 Weafer Street Enniscorthy, www.thewilds.ie. A bright, light-filled café and deli attached to a superb craft shop. Make a beeline here for breakfast, brunch (avocado and poached eggs on sourdough toast, roasted tomatoes and organic leaves or lunch (selection of salads, gourmet sandwiches and burgers). **€**

Dunbrody Country House Hotel Arthurstown, New Ross, www.dunbrodyhouse.com. A blend of classical Irish cooking and continental charm served in the Harvest Room, which overlooks an organic vegetable and fruit garden. The more informal Seafood Champagne Bar serves favourites such as beer-battered fish and chips. **€€€**

WICKLOW

Bridge Tavern Bridge St, Wicklow, http://bridgetavern.ie. Founded in 1759 on the site of an earlier shebeen, this venerable tavern is looking as good as ever, thanks to lots of seductive leather and dark wood filling the spacious, well-lit bars, and a flower-strewn riverside courtyard – here you can enjoy dishes like pan seared rib eye, and Thai spiced salmon with red lentil puree, coconut and broccoli. **€€**

The Happy Pear Church Rd, Greystones, http://thehappypear.ie. A Greystones institution, thanks to its well stocked shop and adjoining café serving organic vegetarian and vegan fare – much of it grown on their own farm – alongside coffee using beans from their own roastery and soda and sourdough breads. **€€**

The Roundwood Inn Main Street, Roundwood, www.roundwood.ie/dining. Roundwood serves great bar meals, ranging from local seafood to delicious Irish stew, as well as dishes such as roast leg of Wicklow lamb in its more formal, weekend restaurant. **€€**

NORTHERN IRELAND

Browns in Town 23 Strand Rd, Derry, http://brownsintown.com. A sleek candlelit city-centre restaurant that showcases the likes of Greencastle seabass and squid, as well as Donegal crab, turf smoked beef, lamb and duck, while for veggies and vegans there is, commendably, a dedicated menu. **£££**

Bushmills Inn 9 Dunluce Rd., Belfast BT57 8QG http://bushmillsinn.com. The smart restaurant, located in the old stables building of this upmarket inn features traditional dishes such as the Botchan (local soup) or Dalriada cullen skink (smoked haddock fillet). **£££**

Deane's Meat Locker 28–40 Howard Street, Belfast BT1 6PF, www.michaeldeane.co.uk. No prizes for guessing what comprises the bulk of the menu here at Michael Deane's classy outfit, and while steak is the main offering, there's much else besides, including seafood chowder, and Korean fried tofu and Asian salad. **£££**

Fish City 33 Ann St, Belfast BT1 4EB http://fish-city.com. Far more than just a fish and chip restaurant, this sparkling little restaurant has all manner of wet treats, from tuna spring rolls to pan roast cod with clam *beurre blanc* plus desserts like red wine poached pear with bergamot curd. **£££**

Harry's Shack The Strand, Portstewart, 028 7083 1783. Boasting an unbeatable beachside location, a beautifully styled interior – raw wood tables and big bay windows – and exquisite food, Harry's ticks all the boxes. Starters might be smoked mackerel fish cakes or shoreline mussels in cider with sourdough, while main course favourites include hake or plaice fresh from Greencastle in Donegal. **£££**

Howard Street 56 Howard Street, Belfast BT1 6PG, www.howardstbelfast.com. This has fast become one of the city's finest restaurants, offering wholesome dishes ranging from beer-battered fish to dry-aged steaks and an excellent range of vegetarian options. **££**

Saltwater Brig 43 Rowreagh Rd, Kircubbin, County Down BT22 1AR, www.saltwaterbrig.com. This family-run pub and restaurant has unbeatable views of Strangford Lough and the Mountains of Mourne. The menu is largely fish-orientated (mussels, salt and chilli squid), but the Sunday roast is very popular. **££**

Travel essentials

PRACTICAL INFORMATION

Accessible Travel 126
Accommodation 126
Airports 126
Apps 127
Bicycle hire 127
Budgeting for your trip 128
Car hire 128
Climate 129
Crime 129
Driving 129
Electricity 130
Embassies and consulates 130
Emergencies 130
Getting there 131
Guides and tours 132
Health and medical care 132
Language 132
LGBTQ+ Travel 134
Money 134
Opening hours 134
Photography 135
Police 135
Public holidays 136
Telephones 136
Time zones 137
Tipping 137
Toilets 137
Tourist information offices 137
Transport 138
Visas and entry requirements 139

ACCESSIBLE TRAVEL

Travellers with disabilities should glean as much information as possible before travelling since facilities in Ireland are generally poor – that said, the number of accessible hotels and restaurants is growing, and reserved parking bays are available almost everywhere, from shopping centres to museums. If you have specific requirements, it's always best to talk first to your chosen hotel or tour operator. The best place to start looking for information is on the joint tourist board website, http://ireland.com/en-us/ahelp-and-advice/practical-information/accessibility. It's also worth consulting the Disability Federation of Ireland (http://disability-federation.ie).

ACCOMMODATION

You'll find accommodation to suit most budgets across Ireland, from swish city hotels and luxurious converted castles to historic country houses and B&Bs; at the very least, most places will offer a continental breakfast but more often than not there's a cooked option. There are also plenty of hostels, varying hugely in quality and atmosphere, but all providing a bed and usually a kitchen, laundry facilities and lounges. Finally, there are well-run campsites and, for the hardy, the chance to pitch a tent in a farmer's field or on common land.

The Irish Hotels Federation (www.irelandhotels.com) and the Northern Ireland Hotels Federation (www.nihf.co.uk) cover numerous hotels and guesthouses across Ireland, with a comprehensive listing, direct booking and special offers available on the website. B&B Ireland (www.bandbireland.com) is the major association of bed and breakfast providers, while the Irish Self-Catering Federation (www.iscf.ie) lists registered providers, including thatched cottages.

AIRPORTS

International flights arrive at Dublin, Cork, Shannon, Knock, and Belfast. Flights also operate from some UK airports to Kerry, Galway, Waterford, Donegal, City of Derry, and Sligo.

Dublin Airport, (www.dublinairport.com) 11km (7 miles) north of the centre. You can get to the centre by Aircoach (http://aircoach.ie), the Dublin Express bus #782 or one of the regular Dublin Bus services, which are slower but cheaper. However, you travel, the trip takes between half an hour and an hour. Taxi time between the airport and central Dublin is also about half an hour.

Shannon Airport (www.shannonairport.com) is situated about 24km (15 miles) to the west of Limerick. The Cork to Galway bus (#51) drops off and picks up at the airport hourly en route to Limerick bus station.

Belfast International Airport (www.belfastairport.com) is 24km (15 miles) west of the city. The 24hr Airport Express 300 bus drops passengers at the city's Europa Buscentre (30–40min).

George Best Belfast City Airport (www.belfastcityairport.com) is handily situated near the city's old docklands, only 5km (3 miles) from Belfast City Centre. The Airport Express 600 bus runs to the Europa Buscentre every 20–35min).

APPS

International taxi apps such as Uber (www.uber.com), Free Now (https://www.free-now.com/ie) and Bolt (https://bolt.eu) are available in Ireland in the major cities, while other useful apps include GoCar (www.gocar.ie) where you can rent a car by the hour and pick it up in various locations across the country. In addition to Google Maps, download the Irish Rail and Transport for Ireland (TFI) apps for timetables, tickets and routes. Given Ireland's unpredictable climate, you'll need to download the Met Ireland app and since exploring major cities requires fuelling, ensure you also have the Deliveroo and Just Eat apps on your phone.

In Dublin, the Leap Card allows you to travel on Dublin Bus, the DART (train) and Luas (tram) – you can add credit to your card using the app, while Dublin Bikes helps you use the popular bicycle rental scheme.

BICYCLE HIRE

Thanks to a rise in insurance premiums, far fewer places in the Republic now rent out bikes – though Dublin now has a city bike scheme – and there are still just a small number of outlets in the North, meaning that it's always wise to book your wheels well ahead. Rental rates are generally around €15–20 per day for a standard bike, roughly double that for an e-bike.

BUDGETING FOR YOUR TRIP

Ireland is by no means a cheap destination, with Dublin by far the most expensive place; indeed it often ranks within the top ten most expensive European cities to visit. Though it's still possible to get a main meal in cafés and pubs for around €10, a three-course restaurant dinner with a glass of wine will usually cost at least €35–40/£30–35, though some offer "early bird" menus and midweek set menus at reduced rates. The price of a pint in a pub is around €4–5, significantly higher in some city-centre clubs.

As a general rule, the minimum expenditure, if you are travelling by public transport, self-catering and camping, would be in the region of €35–40/£30–35 per day, rising to €45–50/£40–45 per day if you're using the hostelling network and grabbing the occasional meal out. Couples staying at budget B&Bs, eating at unpretentious restaurants and visiting the odd tourist attractions are looking at €75–80/£70–75 each per day – if you're renting a car, staying in comfortable B&Bs or hotels and eating well, reckon on at least €140–150/£130–140 a day per person.

CAR HIRE (See also Driving in Ireland)

Outlets of multinational car rental companies, such as Avis and Hertz, can be found at airports, in the cities and in some tourist towns. Rental charges are fairly high – expect to pay around €35/£30 per day plus insurance – though prices are often much cheaper in the Republic than in the North, with the best offers garnered if you book well in advance, especially via the internet. Sometimes smaller local firms can undercut the big names.

In most cases, you'll need to be 23 or over (though some companies may accept younger drivers with a price hike) and able to produce a full and valid driving licence, with no endorsements incurred during the previous two years. If you're planning to cross the border, ensure that your rental agreement provides full insurance; in some cases, you may need to pay extra.

CLIMATE

The Gulf Stream is credited with keeping the Irish weather mild year-round, but the unexpected can happen with readings as cold as -19°C (-2°F) and as hot as 33°C (92°F) recorded over the past century. May is usually the sunniest month of the year, and December the dullest.

Average monthly temperatures in Dublin:

	J	F	M	A	M	J	J	A	S	O	N	D
°F	41	41	43	47	51	56	59	58	56	50	45	43
°C	5	5	6	8	11	13	15	14	13	10	7	6

Temperatures do not vary much from north to south, but the weather in the west and southwest can be a good deal wetter than elsewhere because the winds come in direct from the sea.

In the winter the Wicklow Mountains near Dublin, Donegal in the northwest and County Kerry in the southwest have heavy snowfalls, making the territory dangerous even for seasoned walkers and climbers.

CRIME (See also Emergencies and Police)

Crime in Ireland is largely an urban affair and generally at a low level compared with other European countries. However, thieves do target popular tourist spots, so don't leave anything of value visible in your car and take care of your bags while visiting bars and restaurants. The Tourist SOS service supports tourists who have been the victim of crime, see http://touristsos.ie.

DRIVING (See also Car Rental and Emergencies)

Drive on the left and give way to traffic from the right.

Taking your own car. Be sure to have the registration papers and insurance coverage. Virtually any valid driving licence from any country is recognised in Ireland. If yours doesn't include a photograph, keep your passport with you when driving.

Speed limits. Unless otherwise marked, the speed limit in the Irish Republic is 50kmh (30mph) in towns, 80kmh (50mph) on local roads, 100kmh

(62mph) on national roads and dual carriageways and 120kmh (74mph) on motorways. In Northern Ireland: 30mph (50kmh) in towns, 60mph (86kmh) on local roads, and 70mph (44kmh) on national roads, dual carriageways and motorways.

Fuel. In some areas finding a petrol station open on a Sunday morning may be a problem, so it's best to top up on Saturday for weekend excursions. Petrol (gas) is sold by the litre.

Seat belts. Drivers and front-seat passengers must wear seat belts in the Republic and Northern Ireland; failure to use them may be punished by a fine. If a vehicle is built with rear seat belts, it is compulsory to use them.

Drinking and driving. Random breath tests are used in certain areas. Those who fail risk heavy fines or jail or both.

Road signs. The road direction signs in the Republic are mostly bilingual, in English and Gaelic. Road signs give distances in kilometres in the Republic and miles in Northern Ireland.

ELECTRICITY

The standard electricity supply is 220V AC in the Republic and 240V AC in the North. Most sockets require three-pin plugs. To operate North American appliances you'll need to bring or buy a transformer and an adapter; only the latter is needed for equipment made in Australia or New Zealand.

EMBASSIES AND CONSULATES

Australia: 47–49 St Stephen's Green, Dublin 2; www.ireland.embassy.gov.au
Canada: 7–8 Wilton Terrace, Dublin 2; www.international.gc.ca
Great Britain: 29 Merrion Road, Dublin 4; www.gov.uk
US: 42 Elgin Road, Dublin 4; https://ie.usembassy.gov
In Northern Ireland:
US: Danesfort House, 223 Stranmillis Road, Belfast BT9 5GR; https://uk.usembassy.gov/embassy-consulates/belfast

EMERGENCIES (See also Embassies and Health)

To contact the police, fire department, or an ambulance in the Republic or

Northern Ireland, dial **999 or 112** and tell the emergency operator which service you need.

GETTING THERE

FROM GREAT BRITAIN

By Air. Visitors and tourists can fly in from airports across the UK to Dublin, Shannon, Cork, Kerry, Galway, Waterford, Donegal, Sligo, and Knock in the Republic and to Belfast International, George Best Belfast City, and Derry airports in Northern Ireland. New routes are opening all the time, so it may be worth checking with the airline of your choice for information on the most convenient connections.

Charter Flights and Package Tours. Some airlines offer fly-drive tours, as well as special fares which may include your flight and all the transport to and from your final destination in Ireland. Check with the airline of your choice.

Regional Flights. If your time in Ireland is short, you may consider domestic flights between regions. These are operated by Aer Lingus (www.aerlingus.com).

By Sea. Passenger and car ferries sail frequently from Britain to Ireland. There are services from: Holyhead to Dublin, Liverpool to Belfast and Dublin, Fishguard to Rosslare, Pembroke to Rosslare, and Cairnryan (near Stranraer) to Belfast and Larne (near Belfast).

The main ferry operators include Irish Ferries (www.irishferries.com), P&O (www.poferries.com) and Stena Line (www.stenaline.co.uk). Pets travelling to Ireland or Northern Ireland from the UK require a microchip, valid rabies vaccination, an animal health certificate or a pet passport issued in an EU country or Northern Ireland, and dogs require a tapeworm treatment.

FROM NORTH AMERICA BY AIR

Travellers from almost every major American city and several major Canadian cities can make connections to Dublin, Shannon, Belfast, or Knock, either direct, or via New York, Chicago or Boston.

CHARTER FLIGHTS AND PACKAGE TOURS

Charter flights to Shannon, with connections to Dublin, feature even further air-fare reductions.

GUIDES AND TOURS

Guided tours are conducted at some major attractions as part of the admission fee, and a variety of excursions are led by guides, covering major monuments and attractions by bus. The Tourist Office Dublin at 37 College Green, Dublin 2, tel: (01) 410 0700, www.touristofficedublin.com and **Fáilte Ireland** (www.failteireland.ie) at 88/95 Amiens Street, Dublin 1, tel: (01) 884 7101, have a list of qualified guides. See also www.discoverireland.ie. In Northern Ireland, Discover Northern Ireland (https://discovernorthernireland.com) has itinerary planners.

HEALTH AND MEDICAL CARE

(See also Emergencies)

Visitors from the UK are entitled to medical treatment in the Republic under a reciprocal agreement between the two countries. This will give access only to state-provided medical treatment in the Republic, which covers emergency hospital treatment but not all GPs' surgeries – check that the doctor you're planning to use is registered with the local Health Board Panel. Citizens of some other countries also enjoy reciprocal agreements – in Australia, for example, Medicare has such an arrangement with Ireland and Britain.

In an emergency dial **999** or **112** to find a doctor on call. Pharmacies (chemists) operate during shopping hours. A few stay open until 10pm; in Belfast many are open on Sundays, while in the Republic only some are open for limited hours.

LANGUAGE

English is spoken everywhere in Ireland. In the Gaeltacht areas of the west and south, the principal language is Irish, though everyone can speak English too. Bilingualism is officially encouraged. For short language learning courses in the Gaeltacht, try www.gael-linn.ie or www.liofa.eu.

Here is a short Irish glossary to help you read the signs:

Irish/Gaelic English
Áth ford of river
baile/bally hamlet, group of houses, town
beann/ben mountain peak
cairn mound of stones atop a prehistoric tomb
carrick/carrig rock
cather fort
clachan/clochan small group of dwellings; stepping stones across a river; beehive-shaped hut
corrach marsh or low plain
derry/dare oak tree or wood
donagh church
drum/drom ridge, hillock
dun/doon fort
ennis/inch, innis(h) island
kil, kill, cill church; monk's cell
lough lake, sea inlet
sceillig/skellig crag, rock
sliabh/slieve mountain
tulach/tully hillock

Here are some handy phrases, with a rough guide to pronunciation:

Dia dhuit/diah guich hello
Slán/slawn goodbye
oiche mhaith/e-ha wah good night
go raibh maith agat/goh rev moh a-gut thank you
le do thoil/leh doh hol please
tá fáilte romhat/taw faltcha rowet you're welcome

sláinte!/sloyn-tcha! cheers!
gabh mo leithscéal/gaw mah leshkale excuse me
Cá bhfuil an … ?/koh will on … ? Where is the … ?
fir/mná/fear/min-aw men/women

LGBTQ+ TRAVEL

Ireland's attitude towards the LGBTQ community has come a long way in a remarkably short period of time. A country traditionally seen as culturally conservative, it is now one of the most inclusive and welcoming countries to visit. Being the first country in the world to approve same-sex marriage by popular vote in 2015 wasn't just a huge step towards equal rights, it was recognition of how Irish society has changed. While visitors are unlikely to encounter any trouble, if support is needed, contact http://lgbt.ie.

MONEY

Currency. The unit of currency used in the Irish Republic is the euro (€); in Northern Ireland the British pound sterling (£) is used. Both are divided into 100 units. These units are called cents in the Republic, pence in the north. Euro banknotes are issued in €5, €10, €20, €50, €100 and also €500 denominations. Coins come in 1, 2, 5, 10, 20 and 50 cents and 1 and 2 euro.
Exchange facilities. The best exchange rates are provided by banks, though it's easiest to use an ATM, for which your own bank or credit card company may charge a fixed-rate or percentile fee. Unless you're absolutely stuck, avoid changing money in hotels, where the rates are often very poor. In areas around the border between the Republic and the North many businesses accept both currencies.
Credit cards are widely accepted.

OPENING HOURS

The opening hours of shops and offices can vary from season to season and according to where they are located.
Shops in the cities are normally open from 9am–6pm Mon–Sat and often on

Sunday afternoons; country towns have one early closing day. Big shopping centres often stay open until 9pm on Thu and Fri. Smaller shops, particularly grocers and newsagents, often open on Sun and many stay open until 11pm.

Offices and businesses mostly operate from 9am–5.30pm Mon–Fri. Tourist information offices usually open from 9 or 10am–5pm with longer summer hours in the busiest places.

Banks. In general banks open 9.30am–4pm Mon to Fri in the Republic. Most towns have a late opening day once a week (Thurs in Dublin), when banks open until 5pm. Most remain open over the lunch hour. Northern Ireland banks have similar opening hours, although outside Belfast, branches may close for lunch.

Pubs. In the Republic, the hours are generally 10.30am–11.30pm during the week, with an extra hour Fri & Sat. On Sunday they can open at 12.30pm and stop serving at 11pm. All pubs are closed, by law, on Christmas Day and Good Friday. Pubs in Northern Ireland can apply to serve alcohol until 2am (BST).

Museums and stately homes. Museums and stately homes follow no general rule except that visiting hours will often be curtailed in winter. There are no universal days when these institutions are closed, though Sun, Mon, or Tues are the most probable. To avoid disappointment always check first with the nearest tourist information office.

PHOTOGRAPHY

Be sure to ask permission before you take photos in museums and historic churches; sometimes flash is forbidden. Photography in art galleries is usually not allowed. Military bases (and installations of security forces in Northern Ireland) are off-limits to photographers.

POLICE (See also Emergencies)

The civic guard (police force) of the Irish Republic is the Garda Siochana, known as the Gardai (pronounced 'gorda'). The Police Service of Northern Ireland performs similar duties in the North. In case of emergency, telephone 999 or 112, in both the Republic and Northern Ireland.

PUBLIC HOLIDAYS

Banks and businesses are closed on public holidays, though some shops and restaurants may stay open. If a date falls on a Sunday, then the following Monday is taken in lieu.

IN THE REPUBLIC OF IRELAND AND NORTHERN IRELAND

1 January New Year's Day

17 March St. Patrick's Day

March/April (movable date) Good Friday/Easter Monday

first Monday in May May Day

25 December Christmas Day

26 December Boxing Day

IN THE REPUBLIC OF IRELAND ONLY

first Monday in June June Bank Holiday

first Monday in August August Bank Holiday

last Monday in October October Bank Holiday

IN NORTHERN IRELAND ONLY

last Monday in May Spring Bank Holiday

12 July Orangemen's Day

last Monday in August Summer Bank Holiday

TELEPHONES

Public telephones are increasingly rare but where you do find them, they are marked in Gaelic, *Telefon*. In Northern Ireland, public telephones are found in metal and glass booths or yellow cubicles. They also generally accept coins and cards. Most payphones in Ireland take pre-paid phone cards from local post offices and shops. Dial 10 for operator assistance.

Roaming charges for mobile phones within the EU no longer apply, meaning that UK travellers can use their mobiles throughout the Republic at no extra cost, a situation that looks unlikely to change despite the UK's exit from the EU – that said, check with your network provider for data allowance and charges. Travellers from other parts of the world will need to check whether their phone is multi-band GSM, and will probably also want to find out from their provider what the roaming charges are. The cheapest way to get round roaming charges is to get hold of a UK or Irish pay-as-you-go SIM card to insert in your phone, which will give you a local number and eliminate charges for receiving calls.

The international dialling code for the Republic of Ireland is 353 – drop the initial zero of the local STD code or mobile number. Northern Ireland is 44 as it is part of the UK. The local code for Northern Ireland is 028, from the Republic you can dial 00 44 28 or simply dial 048 followed by the eight-digit number.

TIME ZONES

Ireland sets its clocks one hour ahead of GMT from mid-March to the end of October, but the rest of the year the clocks are set to GMT.

TIPPING

Though discretionary, tipping restaurant staff or taxi drivers is the expected reward for satisfactory service; ten to fifteen percent of your tab will suffice.

TOILETS

Gender signs on doors in the Republic may be printed in Gaelic, not English. *Mná* is Gaelic for ladies; *fir* means gentlemen.

TOURIST INFORMATION OFFICES

Fáilte Ireland (http://discoverireland.ie), as well as the Northern Ireland Tourist Board (NITB; http://discovernorthernireland.com) both provide a wealth of area-specific information on their websites. Abroad, the two boards combine as Tourism Ireland (http://ireland.com). Both provide an extensive network of tourist offices, covering every city, many major towns and almost all the popular tourist areas – in addition, some local councils provide their own offices. Offices are usually open from 9 or 10am–5 or 6pm, although many local ones operate only in the summer.

TRANSPORT

Buses. The state-run Bus Éireann (www.buseireann.ie) operates an extensive network of local, provincial, and express bus routes in the Republic, including full cross-border services in conjunction with Northern Ireland's Ulsterbus Ltd. Services to tourist destinations increases in summer. Expressway buses provide a non-stop inter-city service, while a vast number of private bus companies also operate in the Republic, running services on major routes, as well as areas not covered by the Bus Éireann network.

Dublin Bus *(Bus Atha Cliath)* runs services in the Dublin area. For information, www.dublinbus.ie. Dublin Area Rapid Transit (DART) provides a swift and frequent rail link through the city, from Howth in the north to Greystones in the south. For information on fares and schedules, see www.irishrail.ie/dart. The Luas tram system (www.luas.ie) also provides light rail service to outlying suburbs.

Bus Éireann sell Open Road passes – allowing flexible cross-country travel for varying periods – eg three days out of six, right up to 15 days out of 30. There is also a Rover ticket, which allows up to 15 days of unlimited travel in the Republic, and includes the use of Ulsterbus in Northern Ireland. Or you can buy tickets for combined bus and rail travel: the Explorer pass, for example, is valid in the Republic only.

Trains. Train services in the Republic are operated by Iarnród Éireann (Irish Rail; http://irishrail.ie). Most of the lines fan out from Dublin towards the southern and western coasts, but there are few links between them, and some counties (such as Donegal and Cavan) have no rail links at all. The only line operating between the Republic and the North is the Dublin–Belfast Enterprise service. The North's rail service is operated by Translink (http://translink.co.uk) and restricted to just a few lines running out of Belfast. If your visit to Ireland is just part of a grander European trip, it's well worth investigating the range of different passes on offer, such as InterRail (http://interrail.eu) and Eurail (http://eurail.com).

Taxis. Most taxis park at designated stands waiting for clients. Many towns have radio-dispatched taxis or online booking, but these usually charge extra for the mileage to pick up the client. Fares can vary from town to town. Dublin and Cork have metered taxis while smaller towns have standard fares or charges by agreement.

Note that you should pay only the charge on the meter plus, if applicable, supplements for extra passengers, additional luggage, waiting time, and trips on public holidays or after midnight. An appropriate tip will be appreciated.

Boats and Ferries. With over 4,800km (3,000 miles) of coastline and 14,480km (9,000 miles) of rivers and streams, Ireland is a boater's paradise. You might rent a fishing boat to take advantage of the excellent freshwater and sea fishing, or enjoy the country's scenic splendours in a rented cruiser (normally available with two to eight berths).

No boating permit is needed for travelling on the Shannon, and all companies offer a free piloting lesson. Points of departure include Carrick-on-Shannon, Athlone, Banagher and Killaloe.

The rugged islands off the coast of Ireland are rich in folklore, antiquities and eye-catching natural wonders (especially birdlife). Fáilte Ireland produces a free brochure, *Explore Islands of Ireland* listing numerous possibilities, including scheduled ferries. This information can also be found at www.discoverireland.ie. The Aran Islands are only a 20km (30mile) steamer ride from the Galway coast at Rossaveal, and crossings can also be made in May to September from Doolin in County Clare. Garinish Island, which is noted for its exuberant vegetation, is only ten minutes away from Glengarriff (County Cork). Bad weather may interrupt ferry services. There are connections to the Aran Islands by air, as well; flights are around ten minutes.

VISAS AND ENTRY REQUIREMENTS

Citizens of many countries do not require visas to visit Ireland. EU citizens can enter with a valid passport or national ID card. UK nationals are advised to travel with a passport, but can enter with a valid ID card. However, an immigration officer may ask for proof that you are a UK citizen with Common Travel Area rights. See www.dfa.ie for further information on entry requirements.

If you are coming from outside the euro zone, you must fill in a Customs declaration form for cash sums of over €10,000. For further customs regulations information, visit www.revenue.ie.

Index

A

Achill 87
Aillwee Cave 78
Antrim Coast Road 95
Aran Islands 83
Armagh 98

B

Ballycastle 95
Bantry 69
Belfast 92
  City Hall 93
  Crown Liquor Saloon 94
  First Presbyterian Church 95
  Grand Opera House 94
  Linen Hall Library 93
  Parliament Buildings 95
  Queen's University 94
  Royal Botanic Gardens 94
  SSE Arena 95
  St Anne's Cathedral 95
  St Malachy's Church 95
  Titanic Belfast 95
  Ulster Museum 94
Ben Bulben 88
Blarney Castle 66
Bray 52
Burren, the 77
Bushmills 96

C

Cahir 59
Carrick-a-Rede Rope Bridge 95
Carrickfergus 95
Cashel 60
Castlebar 86
Castletown House 50
Céide Fields 87
Classiebawn Castle 88
Clifden 82
Cliffs of Moher 78
Clonmel 59
Cobh 66
Connemara 81
Conor Pass 74
Coole Park 78
Cork 64
  Cork City Gaol 66
  Patrick Street 65
  St Finbarr's Cathedral 65
Croagh Patrick 85
Curragh 51

D

Derry 97
Derry/Londonderry 97
Dingle 73
Dingle Peninsula 73
Donegal 89
Downpatrick 99
Drogheda 47
Drumcliff 88
Dublin 33, 46
  Bacon, Francis 44
  bars 108
  Chester Beatty Library 40
  Christ Church Cathedral 40
  City Hall 40
  Custom House 35
  Dublin Castle 40
  Dublin City Gallery The Hugh Lane 44
  Dublinia 41
  Dublin Zoo 45
  Four Courts 42
  General Post Office 34
  Grafton Street 37
  Guinness Brewery 46
  Ha'penny Bridge 35
  Irish Museum of Modern Art 45
  James Joyce Centre 44
  Kilmainham Gaol 46
  King's Inns 43
  Leinster House 38
  Marsh's Library 42
  Merrion Square 38
  National Gallery of Ireland 39
  National Museum 39
  O'Connell Street 34
  People's Garden 45
  Phoenix Park 45
  pubs 108
  River Liffey 35
  Royal Hospital 45
  St Michan's Church 43
  St Patrick's 41
  St Stephen's Green 39
  Temple Bar 42
  Trinity College 36
  Wellington Monument 45
Dún Aengus 85
Dunganstown 57
Dún Laoghaire 52
Dunseverick Castle 96

E

Ennis 77

Enniscorthy 55
Enniskillen 98

F
Fermanagh 98
Fort Dunree 90
Foxford 87

G
Galway 79
Cathedral of Our Lady 81
Collegiate Church of St Nicholas 79
Lynch's Castle 80
Salmon Weir 81
Gap of Dunloe 70
Garnish Island 69
Giant's Causeway 96
Glencolumbkille 89
Glendalough 53
Glengarriff 69
Glenveagh National Park 90

H
Holy Cross Abbey 61
Hook peninsula 57
Howth peninsula 46

I
Inch Strand 73
Irish National Heritage Park 55

J
James Joyce Tower and Museum 52
Jerpoint Abbey 62
John F. Kennedy Arboretum 57

K
Kells 49
Kildare 52
Kilkenny 61
Killarney 70
Kinsale 68
Knock 87
Knocknarea 88
Kylemore Abbey 82

L
Larne 95
Limerick 75
Bunratty Castle 76
Hunt Museum 76
King John's Castle 75
St Mary's Cathedral 76
Lisdoonvarna 78
Lismore 59
Lismore Experience 59
Ormond Castle 59
Londonderry 97
Lough Corrib 81

M
Malahide 46
Maynooth 50
Monasterboice 47
Mount Stewart 99
Mourne Mountains 99
Muckross House 70

N
Naas 51
National Stud 51
Navan Fort 98
Newgrange 48
New Ross 57

O
Old Midleton Distillery 67

P
Portrush 97
Powerscourt 52
pubs 115

R
Rathlin Island 95
restaurants 114
Ring of Kerry 71
River Shannon 83
Rosslare 56
Russborough House 54

S
Sandycove 52
Slievemore 87
Sligo 88
St Colmcille/St Columba 49

T
Thurles 60
Trim 49
Trinity College
Book of Kells 37
Old Library 36

U, V
Ulster-American Folk Park 97
Ulster Folk and Transport Museum 99
Varadkar, Leo 29

W, Y
Waterford 57
West Cork Model Railway Village 69
Westport 86
Wexford 55
Youghal 67

YOUR TAILOR-MADE TRIP STARTS HERE

Tailor-made trips and unique adventures crafted by local experts

Rough Guides has been inspiring travellers with lively and thought-provoking guidebooks for more than 35 years. Now we're linking you up with selected local experts to craft your dream trip. They will put together your perfect itinerary and book it at local rates.

Don't follow the crowd – find your own path.

HOW ROUGHGUIDES.COM/TRIPS WORKS

STEP 1

Pick your dream destination, tell us what you want and submit an enquiry.

STEP 2

Fill in a short form to tell your local expert about you dream trip and preferences.

STEP 3

Our local expert will craft your tailor-made itinerary. You'll be able to tweak and refine it until you're completely satisfied.

STEP 4

Book online with ease, pack your bags and enjoy the trip! Our local expert will be on hand 24/7 while you're on the road.

BENEFITS OF PLANNING AND BOOKING AT ROUGHGUIDES.COM/TRIPS

PLAN YOUR ADVENTURE WITH LOCAL EXPERTS

Rough Guides' English-speaking local experts are hand-picked, based on their experience in the travel industry and their impeccable standards of customer service.

SAVE TIME AND GET ACCESS TO LOCAL KNOWLEDGE

When a local expert plans your trip, you save time and money when you book, even during high season. You won't be charged for using a credit card either.

MAKE TRAVEL A BREEZE: BOOK WITH PEACE OF MIND

Enjoy stress-free travel when you use Rough Guides' secure online booking platform. All bookings come with a money-back guarantee.

WHAT DO OTHER TRAVELLERS THINK ABOUT ROUGH GUIDES TRIPS?

This Spain tour company did a fantastic job to make our dream trip perfect. We gave them our travel budget, told them where we would like to go, and they did all of the planning. Our drivers and tour guides were always on time and very knowledgable. The hotel accommodations were better than we would have found on our own. Only one time did we end up in a location that we had not intended to be in. We called the 24 hour phone number, and they immediately fixed the situation.

Don A, USA

PLAN AND BOOK YOUR TRIP AT ROUGHGUIDES.COM/TRIPS

THE **MINI** ROUGH GUIDE TO
IRELAND

Second Edition 2025

Editor: Kate Drynan
Author: Norm Longley
Picture Manager: Tom Smyth
Cartography Update: Katie Bennett
Layout: Grzegorz Madejak
Production Operations Manager: Katie Bennett
Publishing Technology Manager: Rebeka Davies
Head of Publishing: Sarah Clark
Photography Credits: Brian Morrison/Tourism Ireland 53; Catherine Mc Cluskey/Dublin Regional Tourism 44; Chani Anderson 116; Chris Hill/Fáilte Ireland 13T, 14BL, 16BR, 18CL, 64, 91, 92, 93, 98; Corrie Wingate/Apa Publications 36, 38, 41, 73, 75, 76, 87, 89, 103, 112; David Creedon/Fáilte Ireland 16BL; Failte Ireland 13M, 12/13T, 14TL, 14ML; Fáilte Ireland 12B, 12TL, 16TL, 18TL, 18CL, 18BL, 61, 110, 114, 115; G Mitchel 96; Gareth Byrne Photography 35; Glyn Genin/Apa Publications 50, 55, 67, 68, 71; Ireland Tourist Board 47, 48, 79, 80, 82, 100; iStock 32, 43; Kevin Cummins/Apa Publications 94, 105; Liam Murphy/Fáilte Ireland 56, 58; NITB 14BR, 99, 109; Public domain 26; Shutterstock 1, 4, 5, 7, 8, 10, 12CL, 12BL, 13B, 13CT, 13CB, 16ML, 21, 23, 24, 28, 29, 30, 63, 84, 107
Cover Credits: Portmagee, County Kerry
Shutterstock

About the author

Originally from Somerset, Norm has spent much of his working life in Eastern Europe – he is the author of the Rough Guides to Slovenia, Romania and Budapest – but in recent years he has turned his hand to home shores as author of the Scotland, Wales and Ireland guides. These days he divides his time between Orkney and Somerset.

Distribution
UK, Ireland and Europe: Apa Publications (UK) Ltd; sales@roughguides.com
United States and Canada: Ingram Publisher Services; ips@ingramcontent.com
Australia and New Zealand: Booktopia; retailer@booktopia.com.au
Worldwide: Apa Publications (UK) Ltd; sales@roughguides.com

Special Sales, Content Licensing and CoPublishing
Rough Guides can be purchased in bulk quantities at discounted prices. We can create special editions, personalised jackets and corporate imprints tailored to your needs. sales@roughguides.com; http://roughguides.com

Printed in Czech Republic

This book was produced using **Typefi** automated publishing software.

Contact us
Every effort has been made to provide accurate information in this publication, but changes are inevitable. The publisher cannot be held responsible for any resulting loss, inconvenience or injury sustained by any traveller as a result of information or advice contained in the guide. We would appreciate it if readers would call our attention to any errors or outdated information, or if you feel we've left something out. Please send your comments with the subject line "Rough Guide Mini Ireland Update" to mail@uk.roughguides.com.